continuing professional in education

The Learning Classroom

A teacher's guide from Primary to Secondary

Brian Boyd

Series editor: Brian Boyd
Published in association with the
Times Educational Supplement Scotland

HODDER
GIBSON
PART OF HACHETTE LIVRE UK

Although every effort has been made to ensure that website addresses are correct at time of going to press, Hodder Gibson cannot be held responsible for the content of any website mentioned in this book. It is sometimes possible to find a relocated web page by typing in the address of the home page for a website in the URL window of your browser.

Hachette's policy is to use papers that are natural, renewable and recyclable products and made from wood grown in sustainable forests. The logging and manufacturing processes are expected to conform to the environmental regulations of the country of origin.

Orders: please contact Bookpoint Ltd, 130 Milton Park, Abingdon, Oxon OX14 4SB. Telephone: (44) 01235 827720. Fax: (44) 01235 400454. Lines are open 9.00–5.00, Monday to Saturday, with a 24-hour message answering service. Visit our website at www.hoddereducation.co.uk. Hodder Gibson can be contacted direct on: Tel: 0141 848 1609; Fax: 0141 889 6315; email: hoddergibson@hodder.co.uk

© Brian Boyd 2008

First published in 2008 by

Hodder Gibson, an imprint of Hodder Education, part of Hachette Livre UK, 2a Christie Street Paisley PA1 1NB

ISBN-13: 978 0340 946 701

Impression number   5 4 3 2 1
Year   2012 2011 2010 2009 2008

Cover illustration by David Parkin.

Typeset in 10pt Sabon by Transet Ltd, Coventry, England.

Printed in Great Britain by CPI Antony Rowe.

A catalogue record for this title is available from the British Library.

About the author

Professor Brian Boyd is Professor of Education at The University of Strathclyde. He has previously been a teacher of English, a head teacher and Chief Adviser in Strathclyde. He has published widely in the academic press and educational journals, and is a frequent contributor to conferences on a range of educational issues. He is co-founder of Tapestry, an educational organisation whose aim is to promote new thinking about learning and teaching. He used to play on the right wing for Port Glasgow Juniors.

Foreword

The *Times Educational Supplement Scotland* is delighted to be associated with the publication of another book in the Hodder Gibson series dedicated to key areas in the field of continuing professional development.

Since the newspaper's birth in 1965, we have always attempted to inform, educate and, occasionally, entertain the Scottish teaching profession, as well as to encourage dialogue between all educational sectors. In recent years, our commitment to the concept of encouraging educationists constantly to reflect – and act – upon best practice has been most tangibly evident in the special feature on CPD which we run twice a year.

This series of books offers a more permanent testimony of our commitment to CPD. Drawing on the experience of foremost Scottish practitioners, each book attempts to offer academic rigour with a lightness of delivery that is too often found wanting in the weightier tomes that populate many educational libraries, and which are consequently left unread, except by those approaching examinations – or job interviews.

Although we hope these books will be welcomed in the 'groves of academe', we also believe they deserve to be read – and acted upon – by a much wider audience: those teachers across Scotland in the nursery, primary and secondary sectors who deliver the curriculum on a daily basis to our young people.

Neil Munro
Editor, *Times Educational Supplement Scotland*

Contents

The Publishers would like to thank the following for permission to reproduce copyright material:

Acknowledgements pp.22–26 Quotations adapted with the permission of Nelson Thornes Ltd from Essential Teaching Skills – Chris Kyriacou – isbn 978 0 7487 8161 4 first published in 2007; pp.39–45 Material from 'The Highland Council Learning and Teaching CPD Reflection Framework' reproduced with permission of Highland Council; pp. 46–50 Material from 'Embedding a Curriculum for Excellence in the Classroom' reproduced with permission of Highland Council; pp.70 and 176 Extracts from Winnie the Pooh © A.A. Milne. Published by Egmont UK Limited, London and used with permission; pp. 90–93 Extracts from *Education for Citizenship in Scotland* are reproduced with permission of Learning and Teaching Scotland (www.ltscotland.org.uk/citizenship/index.asp); pp. 104–108 Extracts from *The Enterprising School* and pp. 108–110 extracts from *Enterprising Ideas for Secondary Schools* are reproduced with permission of the Centre for Studies in Enterprise, Career Development and Work (Enterprising Careers); pp. 114–115 Extract from 'Learning and Teaching Strategies for A Curriculum for Excellence' reproduced with permission of South Lanarkshire Council; pp. 180 and 131 Extracts from The Tao of Pooh © Benjamin Hoff. Published by Egmont UK Limited, London and used with permission; pp. 161 Extract from The Te of Piglet © Benjamin Hoff. Published by Egmont UK Limited, London and used with permission; pp. 162–168 Extracts from *The Global Dimension in the Curriculum* are reproduced with permission of Learning and Teaching Scotland (www.ltscotland.org.uk/citizenship/index.asp); pp.188 'King Billy' by Edwin Morgan appears in *Collected Poems* by Edwin Morgan, published by Carcanet (1996).

1 Spotlight on the classroom

> What is the point of this teaching of mine,
> and of this
> Learning of theirs? It all goes down the
> same abyss.
>
> **D. H. Lawrence,**
> **'Last Lesson of the Afternoon'**

> And very sweet while the sunlight waves
> In the fresh of the morning, it is to be
> A teacher of these young boys . . .
> **D. H. Lawrence, 'The Best of School'**

Classrooms – from battlegrounds to theatres of dreams

The classroom is an iconic part of schooling. It is instantly recognisable in any country which has a formal education system and it has changed little across the generations. The Scotland Street Museum in Glasgow has preserved three classrooms, from the Victorian era through the First World War to the 1950s, and while the layout changes from tiered rows of benches stretching upwards from the teacher's dais to desks and tables with wooden and then plastic seats, they are all, nevertheless, quite recognisably ... classrooms. They are places where a teacher teaches, and where pupils learn, or not, as the case may be.

Notwithstanding the imaginings of twentieth-century science fiction writers, the twenty-first-century classroom also has four walls, a door, benches or desks or tables and chairs for the pupils and a desk (probably no longer a dais) for the teacher; there will be something for the teacher to put information on, a chalkboard, an overhead projector or, increasingly, an electronic whiteboard linked to a computer; and there may well be material on the walls linked to the learning, posters, pupils' work, reminders of basic rules and content of the subject area(s) to be learned.

There will also be noise from time to time, though, of course, silence may reign. Indeed, there was for a long time a view that silence = order, discipline and learning. Headteachers might patrol the corridors and be uneasy if a classroom was noisy. The sight of young people, 'their round heads busily bowed', as D. H. Lawrence wrote in his more optimistic mood, would signal to the headteacher, and to teachers in Lawrence's day, attentiveness, engagement and absorption in learning. But noise can be purposeful too. Flanders' (1970) 'rule of two thirds' – where, for two thirds of the time in any classroom, there is talk going on; two thirds of the talk is teacher-talk; and two thirds of the teacher-talk is direct influence – may be a more accurate description of the modern classroom. But, in some respects, these are mere details; the classroom, despite momentous changes in society, in technology and even in theories of learning, has remained remarkably constant over the last couple of centuries.

The teacher has remained the focal point of the classroom. Most fictional re-creations, whether in print or on celluloid, have focused on the teacher, normally charismatic, sometimes eccentric, usually under pressure and almost invariably a teacher of literature! The classroom is the stage upon which is played out the drama of motivating 30+ young adolescents. The challenge of raising young eyes and minds beyond the immediate, the mundane, the parochial is one which the hero or heroine normally is able to rise to, often with spectacular success against seemingly insurmountable odds.

For dramatic purposes, the ebb and flow of the teacher–pupil interaction is full of possibilities. For most people who think back on their school careers, it is often the personality of individual teachers which stands out, positively or negatively. The ability of a teacher to have an impact on an individual life – to inspire, to crush, to encourage, to deflate – is legendary.

From 'methodology' to 'pedagogy': $p = m + 2r$

The concept of the 'good teacher' is one which is universally recognised but notoriously difficult to pin down. Everyone has a view – pupils, parents, the public – and research has made its contribution by bringing rigorous analysis to bear on what would otherwise be anecdotal evidence (Boyd, 2005; Rudduck *et al.*, 1996; Cohen, Mannion and Morrison, 2006). Paul Black and Dylan Wiliam and colleagues from Kings College, London (1998) have initiated a programme which, in Scotland, has become a major national development, 'Assessment is for Learning'. Essentially, *Inside the Black Box* (Black and Wiliam, 1998), based on a review of more than 200 pieces of research, world-wide, has begun to focus on the kinds of processes, strategies and methodologies an effective teacher should be using if pupil achievement is to be maximised. It sits well alongside the concept of the 'reflective professional' (Schön, 1983) since the rationale behind the *Assessment is for Learning* initiative is that teachers should understand *why* each of four key aspects of this approach is important. The four key aspects are:

- sharing the learning outcomes with the learners
- extending the range of questioning and dialogue in the classroom
- making feedback formative
- peer- and self-assessment by the learners.

All of these have been shown to improve pupils' learning, and they should be used by teachers who understand *why* they are effective. Thus, the concept of the reflective professional includes being able to make explicit the rationale behind these four approaches. *Methodology* only becomes *pedagogy* when it has a clear rationale and a theoretical underpinning. Thus, the formula

$$p = m + 2r$$

might be helpful: *pedagogy* is *methodology* plus *reflection* and *review*. When teachers can make explicit why they are using particular approaches and regularly review the effectiveness of their teaching, they can be said to have moved beyond methodology towards pedagogy.

The conventional wisdom has been that classroom teachers have no time for theory. Initial Teacher Education is where theory belongs, and the classroom is all about practice, strategies and 'methodology'. And yet there are many theories and ideas out there, and, more importantly, they often find a way into the classroom via curriculum change, new policies or initiatives, often without ever having been made explicit. There are dangers inherent in this 'Trojan Horse' approach to educational theory. If the teachers who are expected to implement the reforms or initiatives are not fully involved in discussion and debate around the theories, the implementation may founder. In Scotland, the introduction of The Primary Memorandum in 1965 did not take teachers along with it and, some 16 years later, Her Majesty's Inspectorate (HMI) bemoaned the pace of change (Boyd, 2005). The gap between the policy-makers and the policy-implementers was simply too great. More insidious, perhaps, is the introduction of new methodologies with no overt link to theory at all. Individualised learning in Mathematics replaced a traditional, text-based, didactic approach in the early 1980s. Supported by HMI, among others, it was sold to the profession as being more child-centred and 'tailored' to individual needs and abilities. However, it took no account of learning theories such as Vygotsky's or Dewey's which emphasised social interaction or the development of thinking. Mathematics classrooms became silent places where pupils worked independently of one another, often on the same work-books or cards, with no real idea why they were doing what they were doing. David Perkins' notion of 'whole game learning' (2008) and Black and Wiliam's (1998) idea of sharing the learning intentions were missing, and teachers had no voice in the discussion.

In recent years, the national policy in Scotland, entitled *A Curriculum for Excellence*, has offered a set of principles for the curriculum:

- challenges and enjoyment
- breadth
- progression
- depth
- personalisation and choice
- coherence
- relevance.

It has also proposed four key purposes:

- successful learners
- confident individuals
- effective contributors
- responsible citizens.

Subsequent publications (e.g. Scottish Executive Education Department, 2006) have sought to offer more practical guidance to teachers using a set of 'curriculum organisers':

- Expressive Arts
- Health and Wellbeing
- Languages
- Mathematics
- Religious and Moral Education (including in denominational schools)
- Science
- Social Studies
- Technologies.

This has been supported by sets of learning outcomes, written in the form of 'I can' and 'I have' statements, from the pupil perspective.

The question now is whether the policy-makers are prepared to engage in an ongoing debate with the policy-implementers about the underlying principles of the pedagogy which should underpin the curriculum change. Full participation in the process will empower teachers and enable them to embed the principles into their practice and to extend their understanding of the efficacy of the strategies which are proposed. Thus, as we will see in Chapter 3, 'Assessment is for Learning' has begun to change not just the things teachers do in classrooms but also the way they think about learning and teaching.

The function of a theory

There is a certain irony in the fact that, given the historical antipathy felt by experienced teachers towards theory (Boyd, 2005), there is now a plethora of approaches, programmes and initiatives, all of which claim a basis in educational theory. As this book attempts to demonstrate, the average teacher now has a bewildering array of approaches claiming legitimacy and, in some cases, absolute Truth. Some approaches seek to command allegiance, while others are offered as a window on the process of teaching for effective learning. Thus it would be possible to look at the learning classroom through a range of prisms: one might take the individual perspective, for example Feuerstein's

Instrumental Enrichment, which offers an all-encompassing philosophical and methodological approach, or one might take a broader *thinking skills* perspective, part of which would be the Feuerstein method (Fisher, 1990). Similarly, while the *Critical Skills Programme* makes impressive claims for its coherent and comprehensive approach, founded on a solid Vygotskian basis (EBD, 1997), others might prefer a more eclectic approach which takes in elements of cooperative learning (Johnson and Johnson, 1990), *Dialogic Teaching* (Alexander, 2004, 2006), *Circle Time* (Mosley, 1993) and collaborative learning approaches.

This book sets out to look at some of the specific initiatives which are challenging Scottish teachers (and teachers world-wide) and considers the implications they have for pedagogy and classroom approaches. It will then attempt to draw from these individual approaches a common set of principles and link them to practices which will help to create a *learning classroom,* one in which the everyday processes, practices and culture ensure that effective learning and teaching for all is taking place.

It will not champion any single approach, nor will it suggest that they are all equally valid. It will offer a critique which may help teachers to construct their own frameworks for assessing the validity of claims made by different programmes. It will look at research evidence, critically, and will consider the somewhat ambivalent relationship between it and practice. If teaching is to be an evidence-based process, what contribution can research make?

School effectiveness and the 'teacher effect'

Since the 1960s, there has emerged a substantial body of educational research on school effectiveness, but, some would argue, the contribution of the individual teacher has been undervalued. To see the teacher as simply one of a number of variables may be more a function of a quantitative research methodology than a case of not seeing the wood for the trees. Nevertheless, for a long time, the emphasis has been on the 'school effect', a statistical concept designed to separate out, in terms of the impact on a young person's achievement, the contribution of an individual school from that of a range of other potential contributory factors such as social class, ethnicity, gender, age, etc. Historically, the 'school effect' has been calculated at around 15% of the total (MacBeath *et al.*, 1996).

However, more recently, Carol Fitz-Gibbon (1997) has argued that the impact that a teacher has on the individual child (the teacher effect) may be up to three times that of the school as organisation. The importance of individual teachers to a young person's life chances may have been acknowledged among the general public (witness the number of magazines which carry a 'My Favourite Teacher' section, often focusing on celebrities of one kind or another), but the research community has only recently identified it as being central to the process of schooling.

Hart *et al.* (2004), as we shall see in Chapter 8, have demonstrated the impact that the teacher can make in the classroom, especially if s/he has tried to create a classroom without limits. By taking the research evidence on intelligence as a concept and on the practice of 'setting' pupils by some measure of prior attainment, the authors seek to demonstrate how teachers who put their principles and belief-systems into practice can create a climate in their classrooms within which all learners become successful learners.

Classroom observation

In his best-selling book, *An Introduction to Classroom Observation*, the late Ted Wragg (1994) succinctly captures the dilemma which has dogged the 'business of classroom observation' (p. viii):

> Skilfully done, classroom observation can be a valuable tool for improving the quality of teaching; badly handled, it can be a menace.
>
> (p. viii)

The purposes of classroom observation include supervision of student and probationary teachers, departmental or school self-evaluation, research, inspection, voluntary sharing of good practice with colleagues, monitoring of aspects of school policy, and so on. But the challenge in Ted Wragg's comments is that each of these purposes changes the nature of the relationship between the observer and the observed. At one end of the continuum is the inspection; here the observed is being judged and has no choice in the matter; s/he may or may not be *au fait* with the criteria being used and may be uncomfortable, anxious and ill-at-ease. The situation is 'high-stakes' since the report on the stage or department or school may be influenced by this single encounter. The observed may feel under pressure to 'perform' in a way which is unnatural in order to conform to what s/he thinks the inspector wishes to see. This we could call the 'accountability' end of the continuum.

At the other end of the continuum is when the observed and observer are in the classroom voluntarily and for a shared purpose. It may be that a new approach in which they both have an interest is being tried, or the observer may be there to see teaching and learning strategies which s/he has never tried but knows are successfully employed by the observed. Here, the observer is more likely to be involved in some way in the lesson, a participant, perhaps helping with pupil activities or taking part in discussion or debate. This is the 'developmental' end of the continuum.

At one school, in an attempt to blur the distinction between accountability and development, the staff began to discuss the practice of 'shared observation'. It was to be on a voluntary basis, and a small committee of staff drew up, for consultation, an *aide-mémoire* which consisted of a checklist of characteristics of good practice in areas such as:

- classroom organisation
- class lesson
- classroom behaviour
- clarity and purposefulness of teacher expositions and explanations
- range and quality of teaching approaches
- pupils as independent learners
- homework
- assessment
- teacher's evaluation of class lesson.

The booklet also contained boxes in which the observer, along with the observed, would write notes after the lesson on:

- observed strengths
- class teacher comments

- agreed areas for consideration
- agreed action points
- staff development needs identified.

The intention was that, once the whole department in this secondary school had participated in these shared observation sessions, a list of departmental teaching strengths and departmental teaching needs would be identified and passed to the staff Learning and Teaching Committee as part of the whole-school attempt to improve the quality of learning and teaching. However, not all schools would necessarily choose to improve the quality of learning and teaching in this way or in such a systematic fashion. One school, where the culture was not so supportive to such a system, agreed that observation would be voluntary, by invitation only and that the philosophy would be 'only feed back positives'. There was to be no identification of 'needs' or 'areas for consideration'. The rationale was that, to build up trust, only strengths would be commented on until the teachers' confidence became such that problems could be raised. Was this 'softly-softly' approach a cop-out, or was it a pragmatic response to a staff wary of classroom observation, perhaps as a result of previous appraisal-linked processes (Boyd, 2005)?

In his Endnote, Ted Wragg tells of a Principal in a New York High School with 7,000 students, regular gang violence and serious drug-related problems.

> Yet every day he could manage it, this Principal, who could have been forgiven for pleading previous engagements, would watch at least one lesson and discuss it with the teacher. Amid all the mayhem, he believed that trying to improve the quality of teaching by joining his colleagues to look at and share the action, was one of the most valuable things he could do, and he was probably right.
>
> (Wragg, 1994, p. 149)

This quotation tells us a lot about the part classroom observation can play in school improvement, and about the life-long quest by Ted Wragg himself to focus on the learning and teaching that takes place in classrooms. This little vignette brings accountability and development together. The Principal in this school must surely have convinced staff that when he came to see them teach it was in the spirit of collegiality and support.

Primary and secondary classrooms: vive la difference?

Boyd (2005) has argued that there are more similarities than differences between primary and secondary school classrooms. Drawing on HMI reports on effective schools, he has suggested that the criteria used to describe effective learning and teaching in each sector are very similar, and, indeed, since the publication *How Good is our School,* now in its third edition (Her Majesty's Inspectorate of Education, 2007), the same quality indicators are used for both sectors.

In *Learning and Teaching in the Primary Classroom* (2007), Maurice Galton explores many of the theories and practices of the primary classroom and does so against the backdrop of what he regards as unhelpful Government policies and initiatives over the previous 10 years. Yet there is little in his table of contents that would not apply to a discussion of learning and teaching in secondary classrooms in the same period:

1 [Primary] teaching in contemporary settings
2 New Labour: New beginning?
3 Learning for teaching
4 Teaching for transmission and understanding
5 Making pupils metacognitively wise
6 Group work in the primary classroom
7 The social and emotional aspects of teaching and other matters

His conclusion is universal, applying equally to primary and secondary schools:

> At the heart of the comprehensive ideal is the need for each school to balance the provision of 'equality of opportunity' for all its students with the need to develop each pupil's 'full potential' … schools must have the freedom to work things out for themselves within the confines of less rigid frameworks of national accountability and testing than currently operate. Only then will schools be able, with confidence, to create the kind of learning communities advocated by Watkins (2005:196) and others where 'the challenge is to create a proactive culture in the classroom' that while it may not 'reflect some aspects of the surrounding culture [can] act as a model of what the surrounding culture might become' (2005:196).
>
> (Galton, 2007, p.127)

Chris Kyriacou, in his widely used *Essential Teaching Skills* (2001), draws no distinction between primary and secondary schools:

> Two major studies of looking at teacher skills have been the Teacher Education Project (Wragg, 1989), which looked at secondary schools, and the Leverhulme Primary Project (Wragg, 1993), which looked at primary schools.
>
> (p. 2)

Yet it must be said that, in most universities which offer Initial Teacher Education (ITE), the courses are separated by sector. Thus there may, in Scotland, be students on a four-year BEd course, students on a one-year postgraduate primary course and students on a one-year postgraduate secondary course, all on the same campus, but with no overlap between the courses, far less opportunities for these students to work together. There may well be many logistical and practical reasons for this separation, but it is ironic that while the most recent curriculum reform, *A Curriculum for Excellence* (Scottish Executive Education Department, 2004), has looked at the 3–18 age range in its entirety, most ITE courses remain self-contained and separate.

The structure of the book

This book is organised around a number of classrooms which a teacher might be expected to create in response to a particular directive or initiative. Each chapter explores an issue, its origin and rationale, considers the advice given to teachers and builds up a picture of what would need to go on in a classroom if the goals of that particular initiative were to be achieved. A critical approach will be taken since teachers are often unable to challenge initiatives and may not always have the time, or the opportunity, to subject every new idea to a critique.

Chapter 2 looks at one of the most vexed and contentious issues in education, and one that surfaces, albeit slightly differently, in every generation, namely, *classroom management*. At the time of writing, there is concern being expressed about the Government's policy on Inclusion and its perceived negative effects on classroom discipline. Many teachers, even those who philosophically believe that all children should be included in mainstream schools wherever possible, are concerned about their ability to cope with large classes which contain pupils with social, emotional and behavioural difficulties (Hamill and Boyd, 2001; 2003). 'The well-managed classroom' considers the evidence from research on Inclusion, including the perceptions of teachers and pupils, and examines the advice offered by Government in its policy paper *Better Behaviour, Better Learning*. This chapter looks at the many approaches which are presented to teachers to help them manage their classrooms more effectively, from *assertive discipline* to creating a positive ethos through praise and rewards.

Chapter 3, 'The formative classroom', builds on the initiative launched in the wake of Black and Wiliam's *Inside the Black Box* (1998). What began as a literature review of the efficacy of 'formative' assessment has developed into a major initiative, in England and Wales as well as Scotland, with a focus on teaching for effective learning. Formative assessment, which has as its focus the improvement of future learning as opposed to the backward-looking 'verdict' of 'summative' assessment, is at the heart of good teaching and learning. The chapter examines why this initiative seems to have caught the imagination of classroom teachers, transforming practice and offering a range of strategies which have been demonstrated to improve pupils' achievement.

Chapter 4 develops the notion of 'The thinking classroom'. The concept of 'thinking skills' has been around for some time. From the writings of educational philosophers such as Dewey, Whitehead and Bruner, through the theories of psychologists such as Piaget and Vygotsky and the programmes developed by Lipman, DeBono, Feuerstein and Adey and colleagues, a growing awareness of the centrality of thinking to the learning process has emerged. Scots such as Nisbet and Entwistle have been at the forefront of introducing concepts such as 'metacognition' into the educational discourse. The debate about thinking skills has revolved around the notions of separate programmes (of which there are many) and 'infusion' through the curriculum, with 'transfer' of skills being the Holy Grail of education. The advantages and disadvantages of each of these approaches are considered and some of the good practice in Local Authorities and schools is examined.

The inclusion of Chapter 5, 'The motivated classroom', in this book is an acknowledgement of the fact that there is a considerable body of psychological literature on this topic and there is a lot of time and energy in Initial Teacher Education and in teachers' Continuing Professional Development (CPD) on this issue. What it is that makes some pupils highly motivated and others not is a complex issue. A range of factors, from pupils' prior attainment, gender, social class and ethnicity to their self-perceptions, the social dynamics of the classroom, the suitability of the curriculum and the role of the teacher are considered. Alan McLean (*The Motivated School*, 2003) offers an interesting analysis of the issue. He has followed up his seminal book with a new publication (2008), which seeks to develop a principled and practical approach for schools.

Chapter 6 considers 'The democratic classroom'. Many countries have long had subjects in their curricula such as 'civics' or 'human relations'. In Scotland, although the Advisory Council of 1944 published a report entitled *Training for Citizenship*, which found references as far back as 1899 to 'instruction ... in the rights and duties of a citizen', no such subject has existed. Indeed, the concept of 'citizenship' has re-emerged in Scotland in recent years as part of the Government's National Priorities (1999). Growing concern about the apathy of the population in general and young people in particular towards the democratic process (as expressed in numbers voting in elections) coupled with what some have described as a 'moral panic' about the behaviour of adolescents in the community, have given the issue of citizenship a new lease of life. This chapter considers the democratic classroom as one which models the key principles of citizenship and looks at the advice that schools have received. Examples of good practice in schools across the country are presented.

Chapter 7 looks at an issue which many would claim to be the issue of the twenty-first century. 'The enterprising classroom' is a modern phenomenon, with many countries, including some of the most economically successful, anxious to retain an edge in an increasingly competitive global market place. The concepts of 'creativity', 'entrepreneurship' and 'enterprise' may be closely linked but they are contested. Not everyone sees them as separate and some might quibble about the values of business and profit-making entering the classroom. However, others would argue that 'enterprise education' is more about changing the culture of schools, making learning serve the needs of the learners and not the curriculum. This chapter looks at these claims, examines the advice given to teachers and looks at the growing body of practice across Scotland.

Chapter 8 looks at another contentious aspect of the classroom, namely whether it is more likely that learners will achieve their potential if organised by some measure of prior attainment in 'sets' or if organised in 'mixed-ability' classes where no prior selection has taken place. That sorting pupils by measures of prior attainment, from tests or examinations to IQ scores, has been the 'default position' for more than a century in many Western countries, is challenged by looking at the growing body of research on the subject. In addition, the kinds of pedagogy which are associated with setting and mixed ability are examined, including the *Learning without Limits* approach (Hart *et al.*, 2004). Strategies which have been found to be successful with classes that are not organised by prior selection are described. *The classroom without limits* is one in which teachers and learners are not inhibited by the application of labels.

Chapter 9 considers the embodiment of the work of Vygotsky in the form of 'The cooperative classroom'. In Scotland, primary classrooms have, since *The Primary Memorandum* (Scottish Education Department, 1965), been places where cooperative learning has always been at the heart of the classroom. In secondary, apart from a brief flourishing in the 1970s and 1980s of 'group work' in some subjects such as English (Boyd, 1979), individualised learning has been the dominant methodology. Of course, some practical subjects such as Art, Home Economics and Technology have always encouraged cooperative learning and Physical Education's emphasis on teamwork has a long history. But the so-called 'academic' subjects tended to have pupils seated as individuals, with didactic teaching predominating, except where practical experiments were being carried out. This chapter looks at recent programmes, including the Canadian Cooperative Learning, the American Critical Skills Programme and the English Dialogic Teaching as well as the more run-of-the-mill small-group learning approaches carried out by teachers across Scotland.

Chapter 10 considers what remains a pivotal concept in Western education, namely *intelligence*. 'The intelligent classroom' is one in which the concept of intelligence itself is explored with pupils. Not only have writers such as Gardner and

Feuerstein helped to re-define the concept from being one-dimensional, fixed, stable over time and with a predictable impact on ability to learn to one which is multi-faceted, 'plastic', malleable and capable of growth, but, more recently, Dweck (1999) has suggested that pupils' *self-theories* or *mindsets* have considerable impact on their learning and their ability to deal with failure. This chapter also looks at *emotional intelligence* and considers how classrooms can operate more effectively by taking account of what we now know about intelligence.

Chapter 11 introduces what might be for some a new concept, namely, 'The global classroom'. Polls have consistently shown that today's young people are concerned about the environment, are interested in world poverty and the plight of the developing world, have strong views on conflicts across the world and have a strong sense of equity and justice. The curriculum in Scotland has tried to keep pace with these issues, and initiatives such as *eco-schools* have been introduced. More recently, Learning and Teaching Scotland, working with aid agencies and other non-governmental organisations (NGOs) has produced a pack on the Global Dimension. This chapter examines these developments and considers what the global classroom might look like.

The final chapter, 'The learning classroom', represents a synthesis of the various perspectives. It examines the principles which underpin the 10 different classrooms highlighted in the book and demonstrates how teachers might create the classroom climate, employ the strategies and methodology and develop the pedagogy which will enable all pupils to become effective learners. The learning classroom is one in which pupils of all abilities are engaged in relevant and challenging learning, motivated to work with others, challenged to think and to reflect on themselves as learners, taking decisions which are based on democratic values and becoming skilled in assessing their own learning and that of others. In the learning classroom, teachers are reflective professionals, sharing their good practice with others, working as part of a team with others who have a stake in their pupils' learning, prepared to work in a range of subject areas in inter-disciplinary ways, as well as separately, and using assessment to promote better learning. This final chapter demonstrates how teachers are already working in this way and suggests what needs to be done to make the quality of learning and teaching consistently high in Scottish schools.

From theory to practice: the essence of pedagogy

The *raison d'être* of this book is to persuade the reader that effective classrooms are not a matter of accident, or an accumulation of intuitive actions, or a mere product of trial and error. For too long teachers have been on the receiving end of 'training' (Boyd, 2005), regarded merely as technicians, being told what to do and how to do it, with little, if any, reference to theory or to research. And yet, there have been many thinkers and writers on education and schooling whose ideas should be considered if not blindly followed. Similarly, there has been for several decades, a steady stream of research on what constitutes effective schools, the results of which have been selectively adopted by successive governments to justify policies as diverse as examination league tables and Inclusion.

This book draws heavily on research, some carried out by the author and a considerable body carried out by others across the world. The intended readership includes reflective professionals, interested and significant others in the education processes, policy-makers and educational leaders. It is intended to be research-led but not research-driven. It looks at theory and at emerging and established practice and attempts to build up a picture of the learning classroom in the twenty-first century. It does not promote any one programme or approach as being the answer to all the problems of pupil underachievement. Rather it looks at a number of important approaches and offers a critique, drawing from them the key underlying principles on which teachers might build their pedagogy.

But what will the classroom teacher make of all of this? From Plato to Piaget, from Binet to Hirst, the ideas of educational philosophers and psychologists have, almost surreptitiously, affected the way in which schools have been conceptualised and curricula organised. Now, in the early part of the twenty-first century, as teachers aspire to be 'reflective professionals' and not mere technicians, as knowledge accumulates of how policy-making needs to engage and empower teachers (Boyd, 2005) and as the stakes involved in ensuring that education is at the heart of enlightened social policy increase, the *why* of effective teaching is more important than simply the *how*.

This book is, unashamedly, about pedagogy, about the complexities of the classroom and about how teachers, working together, reflecting on their practice and empowering learners, can create, wherever they are, 'the learning classroom'.

POINTS FOR REFLECTION

1 Is the concept of *pedagogy* helpful to teachers? Do research and theory have a place in helping teachers to become more effective?

2 How much do you know about how your colleagues teach? What would be the advantages/disadvantages of more *shared observation* among teachers?

3 Do you think the *classrooms* featured in this book are the most relevant ones? Which other classrooms might have been considered?

2 The well-managed classroom

> 'What's wrong with your face, Docherty?'
> 'Skint ma nose, sur.'
> 'How?'
> 'Ah fell an' bumped ma heid in the sheuch, sur.'
> 'I beg your pardon?'. . .
> In the pause, Conn understands the nature of
> the choice, tremblingly, compulsively, makes it.
> 'Ah fell an' bumped ma heid in the sheuch, sur.'
> The blow is instant. His ear seems to enlarge, is
> muffled in numbness. But it is only the dread of
> tears that hurts. Mr Pirrie distends on a lozenge
> of light which mustn't be allowed to break. It
> doesn't. Conn hasn't cried.
> 'That, Docherty, is impertinence. You will
> translate that into the mother-tongue.'
>
> **William McIlvanney,** *Docherty*

Preamble

It is much less likely at this point in history that such an interchange would take place in a Scottish classroom than in William McIlvanney's fictional west of Scotland mining village in the early 1900s. Not only is physical assault, either with a *tawse* or, as in Mr Pirrie's case, the back of the teacher's hand, illegal, but the deliberate confusion of the pupil's use of dialect with 'impertinence' seems almost unbelievable to the modern reader. The exchange between the teacher and the pupil seems brutal, but McIlvanney has captured the complexity and the subtlety of the relationship perfectly. Conn's decision to repeat the reason for his injured face in his own dialect is either foolhardy or brave. He knows that Mr Pirrie's question, 'I beg your pardon?', is not simply a request for clarity. It is a demand that he, Conn, re-phrase the reply, and Conn's fear is palpable. However, his pride, his sense of self-respect, his standing among his peers are all at stake here. Thus, when he knowingly repeats the offending phrase, he, unlike the reader, is not surprised when the blow strikes. The only fear now is breaking down in front of the class. Many teachers who have undertaken training in aspects of 'behaviour management' will recognise the issues at stake here. Indeed, McIlvanney's depiction of this classroom encounter could have come straight out of a manual for newly qualified teachers under the heading *What not to do*. There was a time (when the present writer was at school) when ritual humiliation was part of some teachers' classroom toolkit. But, nowadays, teachers are helped to acquire the skills to avoid confrontation with pupils, especially in front of a class. If a pupil is backed into a corner with no possibility of resolving the situation without loss of face, then it is more than likely he will behave like Conn. At this point of no return, the threat of punishment by the teacher – even the draconian action of Mr Pirrie – is more palatable for the pupil than being humiliated in front of his fellow pupils.

In addition, the demand for the pupil to speak 'in the mother-tongue' seems bizarre in the modern age when the richness of linguistic diversity is more likely to be celebrated than squashed. But, for Mr Pirrie, it was simply another aspect of control and dominance. The 'mother-tongue' in this case is the Queen's English or Received Pronunciation (RP). As recently as the 1980s, the then Secretary of State for Education in the Thatcher Government, John Patten, suggested that pupils' dialects should be 'left at the school gate'. Even Mr Pirrie might have thought this extreme; the classroom door would have been enough for him.

But the biggest difference of all in modern Scottish schools is the absence of corporal punishment. Since the early 1980s, partly as a consequence of a ruling in the European Court, Great Britain abolished the use of corporal punishment in state schools. This decision was no great surprise to most people in education. Effectively it had disappeared from primary schools, and many secondary schools had begun to phase it out. There was much weeping and gnashing of teeth among the general populace, and some sections of the profession foretold the breakdown of civilisation as we know it.

The truth was that, while 'the belt', as it was known in Scotland, had achieved iconic status over the years and most adults claimed that 'It didn't do me any harm', it had never provided a realistic solution to problems of classroom management. The 1977 report on *Truancy and Indiscipline in Scottish Schools* (The Pack Report) had demonstrated clearly that corporal punishment rarely changed behaviour. Indeed, those same people who were seemingly nostalgic about it would admit that the same pupils were belted day after day. Not only that, stories of the injustice associated with the belt abound to this day: whole classes being belted because a culprit would not own up; 'The next person who talks will get the belt' resulting in the meekest, most diligent pupil being punished; and pupils being belted for getting answers wrong in class. And the most terrifying scenario of all for the newly qualified teacher – it happened to the present writer within the first few weeks of teaching – was when the pupil said, simply but defiantly, 'Ah'm no takin' it.'

In this chapter we consider one of the most vexed and controversial issues in education, namely pupil 'indiscipline'. The myths and the reality are considered by looking at the research evidence, including work the present author has carried out. Some of the approaches to dealing with the issue, from *Promoting Positive Behaviour* to *Assertive Discipline,* are considered. The emergence of 'behaviour management' gurus and their advice to teachers are examined. Finally, the views of pupils, teachers and parents, drawn again from recent research (Hamill and Boyd, 2003), are presented.

In this chapter, the focus is on how a well-managed classroom can contribute to the learning environment and how, in turn, an appropriate pedagogy can contribute to good behaviour.

Discipline

Discipline has been, and continues to be, the most contentious issue in education. Every generation of teachers seems to believe that standards of pupil behaviour have fallen. Perceived causes vary, ranging from the breakdown of respect in society to the disintegration of the nuclear family. In more recent years, the drug culture, the internet and increasingly materialistic, consumerist society, have been blamed. Some causes are transient, only to be replaced by others, more sinister; television, rock music and computer games are of that ilk, surely to be overtaken by the next technological advance or teenage craze. Within schools themselves, the abolition of corporal punishment and the policy of Inclusion are felt by many to be contributory factors in the deterioration of discipline in our schools.

The press, educational and popular, regularly run stories on this subject, sometimes occasioned by specific events (such as the assault on a headteacher by a pupil, captured by his friend on a mobile phone camera and posted on the internet) or by the publication of statistics on 'physical violence and verbal abuse' each year. The educational press normally reacts to these issues with a balanced view, but even here we can see opposing views championed. Ewan Aitken, formally convenor of the Education Committee in Edinburgh Council, is a doughty champion of Inclusion. His fellow columnist in the *Times Educational Supplement Scotland*, Marj Adams, a teacher of Religious Studies, Philosophy and Psychology, regularly takes a harder line on issues of discipline. Her article 'Denial worse than the abuse' (Adams, 2007) looks at three unrelated issues, namely the legal action launched by a teacher seeking compensation for 'unruly pupil behaviour', an attack on the home of two teachers by pupils with missiles on Hallowe'en and the publication of statistics for 2006–2007 of incidents of pupil violence or verbal abuse (some 7,000). Her view is that 'standards of behaviour continue to deteriorate'. She supports her argument by 'an internet trawl of references to violence in the classroom' and by reference to the *Times Educational Supplement Scotland* online staffroom forum.

Adams is of the view that 'School, unlike many other areas of life, would appear to tolerate practically any kind of behaviour, with the offender receiving much more attention than those whom he is affecting.' Towards the end of the article, there is an acknowledgement that it is only a 'small minority of pupils whom no-one can reach' and a final, ironic comment on the lack of parenting skills among the population.

It is important to realise that this kind of writing represents a strand of thinking among the teaching profession and the population at large. It would be easy to counter most of the arguments in the article. A figure of 7,000 instances of physical or verbal abuse (there is no indication of how many of each) seems high until we remember that there are 3,000 schools in

Scotland and that pupils attend for some 190+ days. The fact is that some schools will hardly ever experience such incidents while others, especially those serving areas of social disadvantage, may have more. And, for every story of teachers suffering harassment in their communities, there are many more where they live harmoniously among their pupils and their families. That parenting is often inadequate is a fact; it has always been thus.

Adams is right to remind us that schools are often the last bastions of values in a society which seems increasingly fragmented. But to suggest that they 'tolerate practically any kind of behaviour' is simply not true. What is undoubtedly true is that, when they do invoke sanctions when pupils misbehave, they can no longer rely on the unequivocal support of parents, as they might have done a generation ago. Thus, the point of agreement among those who favour inclusion and those who see some pupils as unreachable is that society has changed and that the job of schools and teachers has been made more difficult as a consequence.

Sources of advice to teachers

Most teachers receive their first advice on classroom management during Initial Teacher Education (ITE). Two of the most widely used textbooks are *Essential Teaching Skills* (Kyriacou, 2007) and *A Guide to Teaching Practice* (Cohen, Mannion and Morrison, 2004), and each has a section on this issue.

Kyriacou's *Essential Teaching Skills*

Kyriacou's chapter on discipline opens with the observation that 'order is needed in the classroom if the activities which take place are to facilitate effective learning by pupils' (p. 83). He takes a positive stance on how order can be achieved:

> ... creating the necessary order is more to do with the skills involved in effective teaching in general than it is to do with how you deal with pupil misbehaviour itself.
>
> (p. 83)

He argues that if the learning and teaching are well-planned, challenging, engaging and appropriate, then misbehaviour is less likely to occur. He might well concur with the present author that the Scottish Executive's 2001 report on this issue, *Better Behaviour, Better Learning*, got things the wrong way round. Kyriacou argues that 'skilful teaching . . . lies at the heart of establishing discipline'.

However, it is a fact that, no matter how effective your teaching is, there will be misbehaviour from time to time. Kyriacou suggests that 'most pupil misbehaviour is quite trivial'. But it is often this kind of low-level misbehaviour which most undermines teachers' good intentions. Kyriacou outlines a number of *causes* of pupil misbehaviour, from boredom to inability to do the work, from low academic self-esteem to a lack of negative consequences. His advice to emerging teachers is to focus on a number of key areas including: establishing your authority; pre-empting pupil misbehaviour; and using reprimands and punishments.

Establishing your authority

Teachers who have exemplary classroom management tend to be 'relaxed, self-assured and confident' (p. 87). These qualities are conveyed through a subtle mix of voice, body-language and posture. Observing experienced teachers operate is, perhaps, one of the most useful kinds of CPD, looking at how they create a climate in which their authority is taken for granted, where they rarely, if ever, shout and where they are often a part of the learning, perhaps sitting with a group, with no detriment to their overall status. The rules of engagement in the classroom should be negotiated, fair and equitable, and reinforced on a regular basis.

Pre-empting pupil misbehaviour

Kyriacou's list of 'do's' for teachers is interesting:

- Scan the classroom
- Circulate
- Make eye contact
- Target your questions
- Use proximity
- Give academic help

- Change activities or pace
- Notice misbehaviour
- Notice disrespect
- Move pupils

(p. 90–1)

These are recognisable as the kinds of advice more experienced teachers have given to students. But, in the light of other chapters in this book, the list does look rather teacher-centric, assuming that it is the teacher's role alone to focus on behaviour. Much of the current thinking on this issue would point to pedagogies which would have the pupils more actively involved in the creation of good working conditions within the classroom. A good example would be 'Target your questions'; rather than put the onus on the teacher, perhaps an alternative approach would be to train pupils in a range of protocols for discussion, small-group and whole-class, and begin to shift the responsibility to them for the maintenance of good order. Similarly, 'Move pupils' should really only be a last resort if the groups have been formed purposefully, the roles agreed, the responsibilities accepted and the tasks appropriate. Kyriacou's observation that 'seating arrangements are a privilege rather than a right' (p. 91) is, perhaps, taken care of if the pupils are involved from the outset in decisions about seating and the relationship between how and where they sit with the learning which is to take place.

Using reprimands and punishments

Kyriacou deals with these problematic issues in a very matter-of-fact way. He advises that reprimands be used sparingly, because of a law of diminishing returns. He offers another list, this time of pointers to the effective use of reprimands:

- Target correctly
- Be firm
- Express concern
- Avoid anger
- Emphasise what is required
- Maintain a psychological impact
- Avoid confrontations
- Criticise the behaviour of the pupil
- Use private rather than public reprimands

- Be pre-emptive
- State rules and rationale
- Avoid making hostile remarks
- Avoid unfair comparisons
- Be consistent
- Do not make empty threats
- Avoid reprimanding the whole class
- Make an example.

(pp. 94)

The problem here is that there are simply too many suggestions. Most of them are sensible and borne out by experience: 'avoid reprimanding the whole class'; 'avoid anger'; 'state rules and rationale'; etc. However, some of the others are problematic, for example, 'maintain psychological impact' seems to be more about dominance than anything else, and 'make an example' runs the risk of escalation or of picking on one pupil *pour encourager les autres*. Kyriacou's most telling piece of advice is to remind us that frequent misbehaviour may be 'an on-going critique by the pupils of the demands made upon them' (p. 96). Kyriacou's section on punishments begins with a definition: '. . .a formal action which the pupil is intended to experience as unpleasant, as a means of helping the pupil to behave appropriately in the future' (p. 96). He looks in turn at three purposes of punishment: retribution, deterrence and rehabilitation. However, he is at his most perceptive when he deals with the 'shortcomings of punishment' (p. 97):

- They form an inappropriate model for human relationships.
- They foster anxiety and resentment.
- They have a short-lived 'initial shock' effect.
- They encourage pupils to develop strategies to avoid getting caught.
- They do not promote good behaviour directly but simply serve to suppress misbehaviour.
- They do not deal with the cause of the misbehaviour.
- They focus attention on the misbehaviour.

(p. 97)

He considers, in turn, a long list of common punishments, from lines to detention, from loss of privileges to exclusion (from class and from school) but concludes, as did teachers in a survey conducted for the Elton Report (1989), that 'strategies based on reasoning with pupils are the most effective' (p. 99).

His final section, on dealing with confrontations, is brief. Essentially, it is best to avoid them, or try to defuse them or get help. These should never be seen as a win-lose situation by the teacher and, by using your superior social skills, it is almost always possible to avoid the situation escalating, especially if there is an 'audience' present. If the teacher is aware of his/her own role in such a situation, is prepared to look for solutions rather than victory at that point, the confrontation can usually be avoided and the issue dealt with later. This chapter began with a fictionalised account of a confrontation in which both parties made conscious decisions *not* to avoid escalation, and there was only one winner in the power struggle. But it could be argued that Mr Pirrie was the real loser; at least Conn emerged with a modicum of dignity.

(Quotations adapted with the permission of Nelson Thornes Ltd from Essential Teaching Skills – Chris Kyriacou – isbn 978 0 7487 81614, first published in 2007.)

Cohen *et al.*'s *A Guide to Teaching Practice*

The Cohen, Mannion and Morrison book is widely used in Initial Teacher Education. It has a substantial section on 'Management and Control in the Classroom' (pp. 281–335); it makes the point at the outset that this is a complex issue and that a range of 'complex factors' comes into play, including:

- preparation and planning
- suitability of material
- teaching methods
- teacher–pupil relationships.

(p. 281)

The authors take the view that 'discipline' must be 'built-in' rather than a 'bolt-on' element. They refer to the Elton Report (1989), which argued that good behaviour and good teaching cannot be separated (Cohen *et al.*, 2004, p. 283).

In a chapter which is a helpful blend of the theoretical and the practical, Cohen and colleagues deal with an issue which brings together classroom organisation and discipline, namely 'Rules and Routines'. They suggest that 'Educational settings have traditionally featured too many rules, especially punitive ones' (p. 308) and support this with three reasons:

1 The number of disciplinary actions a teacher takes is kept to a minimum.
2 Rules contribute to stultifying the atmosphere of ... a classroom.
3 Rules themselves exert little influence on classroom behaviour.

(p. 309)

They suggest three key principles which should underpin classroom rules: relevance, meaningfulness and positiveness.

Relevance

Rules will vary according to the class and to the context of lessons. Therefore, flexibility rather than rigidity is required.

Meaningfulness

Arbitrariness is unhelpful when it comes to classroom rules. Rules should make sense to all concerned. The concepts of 'right', 'proper' and 'sensible' should be clearly understood by the pupils.

Positiveness

Cohen and colleagues suggest that rules should be expressed in terms of Do's rather than Don'ts where possible. Many of the rules will be about the routines of the classroom while others will concern relationships. The principles will be established early in the teacher's relationship with the class while the details will be built up over time as situations arise.

Induction of new teachers

There has existed a tension in the past between what the teaching profession believes is necessary in terms of classroom management and how they believe that Initial Teacher Education (ITE) prepares emerging teachers. Put simply, ITE is often thought to be overly theoretical, somewhat liberal and, bluntly, out of touch with the 'real world'. However, if Cohen and colleagues' analysis is the basis of much of what takes place in ITE, would experienced teachers be reassured?

In summary, good classroom management involves establishing clear rules where rules are needed, avoiding unnecessary ones, eliminating punitive ones, reviewing them periodically, and changing or dropping them when appropriate. Additionally, greater flexibility may be introduced by having recourse to more informal arrangements, frequently arrived at by negotiations and bargaining.

(p. 310)

Finally, they make the link between rules and routines before going on to rewards and punishments. This section of the book concludes emphatically with a section on teacher's expectations, and the authors cite Good and Brophy (1974) who argued that the most influential element of classroom management is the teacher and her/his expectations of the learners, shared with them and consistently reinforced over time. The key concept is *respect*, and teacher–class relationships built on respect are likely to be positive.

Programmes and approaches

There are a number of approaches to discipline available to schools and to teachers. Cohen *et al.* deal briefly with *Assertive Discipline,* an American approach which has gained in popularity in Scottish schools in recent years. Another approach which has been introduced is *Win-Win Discipline* by Spencer Kagan *et al.* (2004), presented in a compendious volume and derived from their work on cooperative learning.

An approach which has found favour in primary schools and which is beginning to make inroads into secondaries is *circle time.* Jenny Mosley's highly successful book *Turn Your School Round: A Circle-Time Approach to the Development of Self-Esteem and Positive Behaviour in the Primary Staffroom, Classroom and Playground* (1998) has a foreword by Lord Elton and contains a section on the classroom. There are structures, ideas and games as well as opening and closing activities. The approach is practical, positive and based on relationships.

The key issue with programmes and approaches is that they are often based on psychological and/or philosophical conceptions of the classroom and the ways in which human beings interact. Thus while one approach might be heavily *behaviourist* and based on the consistent application of pre-specified rules with cumulative sanctions applied to misdemeanours, another will major on relationships, social interaction and pupils' internalisation of the expectations of the teacher.

It is unlikely that any one programme will cover every situation, and all run the risk of becoming too prescriptive or dogmatic. They key is for teachers to *understand* the probable causes of indiscipline and to be aware of the role which their management plays in creating a classroom culture which is inclusive and positive. As McLean (2003) observes, motivation is the 'new discipline' (see Chapter 5). A focus on rules and punishments may ignore the root causes of classroom misbehaviour and may therefore make lasting solutions more difficult to achieve.

Sectoral differences: a question of architecture?

The present author has written elsewhere about the differences and similarities between primary and secondary schools (Boyd, 2005). In the context of the well-managed classroom, it has to be acknowledged that classrooms do not exist in isolation from the school as a learning community. While it is accepted that whole-school philosophies, policies and ethos are hugely influential in what happens in classrooms, it is also true that school structures, the curriculum and contextual factors can impinge on classrooms and affect significantly the way in which teachers and pupils experience the education process.

Thus, the fact that the school day can be more flexibly organised in early years, primary and additional support needs schools, means the relationship between teacher and class or group is more likely to be consistent and lasting, the learning episodes can be adapted in terms of length of time, location and content to suit the demands of the curriculum and the needs of the pupils, and so on. The key here is the potential for flexibility and the close relationship between teacher and learners.

In the secondary school, the constant changing of periods, every 50 minutes, six or seven each day, with whole classes of pupils in a gigantic pin-ball machine, bouncing from one extremity to the other, causing congestion in the stairwells and corridors, and inevitably arriving late for the next class, is a common feature. If the school has more than 1,800 pupils (a more common occurrence now than 10 years ago because of mergers required by Government to finance new school buildings), the result can be a system which does little to facilitate good order and a sense of belonging. In fact, these schools and their staff work hard to mitigate the worst effects of this aspect of curriculum architecture, but school size, length of lesson and the shape of the school day all play a part in how learning is experienced by pupils.

These aspects of curriculum architecture, along with issues of class size, class organisation (setting) and whether curriculum is seen as subject centred or inter-disciplinary or both, are all pertinent to the issue of classroom management. In the secondary school, having seven classes in one day, in different rooms, sometimes with minimal relevant dedicated resources, all make it difficult to create a classroom climate which is conducive to a well-managed classroom. If the class is a bottom set, with curriculum content which appears less than relevant and if there is no support for those young people whose behaviour is challenging, then classroom management is often the only focus of the lesson.

In the primary school, it would appear that the curriculum is emerging from almost 20 years of the 5–14 programme where each subject area was allocated a precise percentage of the total time available each week (Boyd, 2005), where forward plans were rigid and inflexible and where the teacher had little room to manoeuvre in terms of 'going with the flow' in a particular topic. Through *A Curriculum for Excellence,* there is now a greater possibility of tailoring the curriculum to suit the needs of pupils, of breaking free of arbitrary Levels (which too often became labels) and joining up pupils' learning wherever it is appropriate.

There is growing evidence that the divide between primary and secondary (and nursery and primary) can also be ameliorated by using the flexibility referred to above. Increasingly, clusters of schools (normally the nurseries, primaries, additional support needs and their associated secondary school) are forming themselves in to Learning Communities so that the curriculum can be planned in a holistic way for the 3–18 age group. The sharing of expertise and staff across the sectors may well enable classroom management to become an area in which staff can share expertise and on which in-house CPD is focused. The solutions to the problems of classroom management are, in a real sense, available to teachers through the accumulated expertise of their colleagues, if there is time, and opportunity, for sharing to take place.

Better learning, better behaviour

It has long been the view of the present writer that the Scottish Executive's report of the Discipline Task Force, *Better Behaviour, Better Learning* (2001), put the cart before the horse, so-to-speak. The reasons for this may well have been political; after all, the chair of the group was Minister for Education and the impetus for the establishment of the Task Force was, as he wrote in his Foreword, 'the level of concern' expressed by teachers during the recent negotiations on pay and conditions of service, about 'pupil indiscipline'. The Minister had to be seen to react and he did so in the time-honoured Scottish way by gathering together representatives from all strands of Scottish education.

The presence in the group of distinguished educationists ensured that the link between learning and behaviour was not lost; indeed, the first of the 36 recommendations of the Task Force was that there should be more 'curriculum flexibility' to allow schools to meet local and individual needs. Later in the document the point is made that discipline cannot be separated from learning and teaching because the two are 'inextricably linked' (p. 8). But the report is a formal one, organised in numbered paragraphs and written in civil servant-ese. Nowhere, not even in the section headed 'Effective learning and teaching' (pp. 18–19) is there any in-depth analysis of how people learn and how pedagogy might take account of this. Instead, there is the briefest of references to the concept of 'differentiation' without any serious attempt to discuss its complexity, and a superficial reference to one aspect of the contested idea of 'learning styles' (Coffield *et al.*, 2004).

It is hardly surprising, therefore, that the headline actions emanating from the Government report were things like the allocation of funding to secondary schools to established *bases* for disruptive pupils, even though not all schools wanted them, (Hamill and Boyd, 2001). Thus, while 'The importance of high quality learning and teaching' was one of the 'key themes' of the report, some £30 million was allocated over three years by the new Minister for Education, Cathy Jamieson, to be spent on bases, classroom assistants and home-link workers. Politically, the link between learning and indiscipline receded as resourcing became the key Government focus.

Until the issue of classroom management and pupil indiscipline are seen as part of the complex of factors which surround learning and teaching within schools, there is always the danger that policies are created either as knee-jerk responses to concerns expressed (from whatever quarter) or as attempts made to deal with the symptoms rather than the causes. All of the recommendations of *Better Behaviour, Better Learning* were well-intentioned, but they failed to put learning at the heart of the matter, relegating it instead to one of a list of eight key themes.

Principles of the well-managed classroom

It seems clear that whatever the manifestations of challenging behaviours in the classroom, the causes are often complex and the solutions difficult. It is difficult to imagine how every teacher could be expected to be able to meet the needs of every child in every class without support and guidance from others, including the other pupils.

The principles which emerge from the literature and from teachers' practice are:

- *Relationships* These are key to a well-managed classroom: mutual respect, unconditional positive regard and a refusal to label individuals, by gender, background, 'intelligence' or, indeed, by any criteria. In the words of pupils, a good teacher 'has faith in you' and 'makes you feel clever' (MacBeath *et al.*, 1996). A classroom built on respect will be one less likely to be conducive to misbehaviour.
- *Consistency* It is often said that children and young people respond best when they have clear limits. When interviewed, pupils often refer to this, suggesting that in their view a good teacher is one whose classroom is well-organised, fair and one in which the teacher 'has time for you'. Time is always at a premium when there are 30 (or even 20) pupils in a class. Thus, time spent at the beginning of the year, discussing, negotiating and reinforcing class rules and protocols with the pupils will save time throughout the year by not having to deal with frequent, low-level misbehaviour.

- *Self-discipline* The goal of any teacher must be to encourage self-discipline in pupils. The ability to control impulsivity, to think of the consequences of words and actions, to work towards medium- and long-term goals and to discuss and cooperate with others with whom you may disagree, is not natural and innate. Pupils need to be supported in the development of such skills, and the mediation of the teacher, other adults and pupils is crucial. The key elements are trust and transparency; pupils need to be sure that when others are curtailing their behaviour they are doing so according to criteria which have been shared and which they understand.

POINTS FOR REFLECTION

1. What are your main concerns about discipline in classrooms nowadays?

2. What do you think of the advice given to trainee teachers in the books used in ITE?

3. What are your views of the principles of *the well-managed classroom*?

3 The formative classroom

> 'I only took the regular course.'
> 'What was that?' enquired Alice.
> 'Reeling and Writhing, of course, to begin with,' the Mock Turtle replied; 'and then the different branches of Arithmetic – Ambition, Distraction, Uglification and Derision.'
> 'I never heard of "Uglification,"' Alice ventured to say.
> 'What is it?'
> The Gryphon lifted up both its paws in surprise. 'Never heard of Uglifying!' it exclaimed. 'You know what to beautify is, I suppose?'
> 'Yes,' said Alice doubtfully: 'it means – to – make – anything – prettier.'
> 'Well, then,' the Gryphon went on, 'if you don't know what to uglify is, you are a simpleton.'
>
> Lewis Carroll, *Alice's Adventures in Wonderland*

Inside the black box

Few working in the field of education could have anticipated the impact of a rather slight digest of a literature review carried out by two academics from King's College in London and their colleagues. *Inside the Black Box* by Paul Black and Dylan Wiliam (1998) consists of 21 A5 pages, including a page and a half of references. The *black box* of the title is the classroom and the focus of the document is *formative assessment*. However, the authors are adamant that formative assessment is not an end in itself; rather 'it is at the heart of effective teaching' (p. 5). Indeed, they make it clear that:

the term *assessment* refers to all those activities undertaken by teachers, *and by their students in assessing themselves,* which provide information to be used as feedback to modify the teaching and learning activities in which they are engaged.

(p. 2)

The authors pose three 'important questions' about the process of formative assessment (formative assessment defined as being 'when the evidence is actually used to adapt the teaching work to meet the needs'):

• Is there evidence that improving formative assessment raises standards?
• Is there evidence that there is room for improvement?
• Is there evidence about how to improve formative assessment?

(p. 2)

The scope of the evidence which underpins their answers to these three questions is impressive. 'Many books' and all of the issues of some 160 journals over a nine-year period yielded some 580 articles or chapters. More than 250 of these were used in the preparation of the publication and the entire review was published in the journal *Assessment in Education* (Black and Wiliam, 1998c).

In short, the answer to each of their three questions is 'Yes'. Their findings, which suggest that formative assessment improves learning in ways which are measurable, are taken from studies involving learners from the age of five to those at university. The authors, helpfully, include a little seminar on research methodology, informing the reader that:

... the average improvements in pupils' scores on tests ... [divided by] ... the range of scores that are found for typical groups of pupils on the same tests ... is known as the *effect size.*

(p. 4)

They go on to tell us that the effect size in these studies that they cite range from 0.4 to 0.7, 'larger than most of those found for educational interventions' (p. 4). What is remarkable for a publication such as this is that such technical detail is rarely included for a wider audience. However, it is almost certain that it is this very evidence-base which has helped to give *Inside the*

Black Box such credibility. The reader is being taken seriously and not patronised.

A further important piece of evidence presented is that 'formative assessment helps the (so-called) low attainers more than the rest' (p. 4). This, the authors argue, is particularly important since so-called low attainers often become disillusioned with school and cause disproportionate numbers of challenges for the system. Black and Wiliam argue that 'new modes of pedagogy' are called for, including pupils' active involvement in their learning, assessment information used to adjust learning and teaching programmes and self-assessment as a way to improve motivation and enhance learning.

Their evidence suggests that many of the previous assessment practices were 'beset with problems and shortcomings' (p. 5). They argue that many assessment practices fail to promote *effective learning* by focusing on rote learning rather than understanding and by concentrating on quantity rather than quality of pupil work. They go further and argue that assessment can sometimes have a *negative impact* by emphasising the giving of marks rather than useful advice and by giving precedence to the comparison of pupils with one another, with consequential de-motivation of those who feel they lack ability. Finally, they are critical of the *managerial role* of assessment, linking it to exams, trying to predict future success by giving tests which mirror external exams and by spending more time collecting marks than analysing pupils' work.

Black and Wiliam, critical of the UK Government's apparent lack of commitment to formative assessment, with the emphasis on Standard Assessment Tests (SATs), Key Stages and examination results, went on to look at the evidence about 'how to improve formative assessment' (p. 8). Their first focus is on the *self-esteem of pupils*. Here, they were, controversially for the time, critical of classroom cultures that focused on 'rewards, gold stars, grades or place-in-the-class ranking' (pp. 8–9) which encourage pupils to focus simply on getting good marks rather than on becoming better learners. These pupils, claim Black and Wiliam, learn to 'avoid difficult tasks' where they have any choice, looking only for the 'right answer'. If they get poor results they conclude that they have low ability and give up and they attribute these difficulties to factors outwith their control. They fear failure and often turn their energies to disruptive behaviour.

Black and Wiliam suggest that pupils of high ability thrive in such a culture, but that view has been challenged by Carol Dweck in her book *Self-Theories* (1999) and in her later work. Her focus is on intelligence and in particular the learner's perception of her intelligence. If the learner believes intelligence to be fixed, unalterable, stable over time and predictive of future success, then, argues Dweck, she will give up when problems arrive, will attribute lack of success to lack of ability and will often give up subjects because she believes that she just isn't good at them. Recently, Dweck has referred to this approach as a 'fixed mindset' and has suggested that it is prevalent among 'able' learners who have not learned to deal with 'failure'.

Dweck suggests that if learners are encouraged to see intelligence as malleable, as capable of growth in the same way as the brain itself can grow and only one of a number of factors contributing to successful learning (others being hard work, having a range of strategies, motivation, etc.), then when they hit a problem they are much more likely to re-group, seek other solutions and, above all, stay positive about their abilities. Dweck calls this a 'growth mindset'. She argues that more able learners who are educated in a culture of marks and rank-ordering are, in fact, more likely to have a 'fixed mindset' and to try to avoid failure.

What links the Black and Wiliam analysis to Carol Dweck's work is not this difference about the reaction of more able learners to failure, but their agreement that the emphasis should be on what Entwistle referred to as 'deep' rather than 'surface' learning. They call for a 'culture of success' to be created in the classroom. Where Black and Wiliam and Dweck seem to be at one is that 'self-esteem' is not simply a warm-and-fuzzy concept, a feel-good factor. Indeed, Dweck is worried about the wrong kind of praise being used in the classroom. She prefers the term 'self-efficacy' to self-esteem, because it places the learner in control. The job of the teacher is to praise effort not intelligence, to focus on the process of learning not simply the product. Black and Wiliam suggest that formative assessment has the same effect, focusing on the process of learning and giving the pupil a clear understanding of what s/he needs to do to learn more effectively. They warn against feedback which is 'clouded by overtones about ability, competition and comparisons with others' (p. 9).

The area of *self-assessment by pupils* is an important one, but one which teachers have traditionally found difficult to implement. There are many objections which can be raised by teachers who are sceptical about pupil self-assessment as a viable classroom strategy. The most common is the assertion that pupils, of whatever age, are not trustworthy and are incapable of reliable self-judgement. Others will claim that self-assessment by pupils is simply too time-consuming and it is more economical of time for the teacher to take home the jotters, do the marking and give it back to the pupils later. Finally, it is not uncommon to find teachers who say that self-assessment is simply unnecessary; it's the teacher who has the superior expertise and is therefore best placed to assess pupils' work. For Black and Wiliam, these objections are simply smokescreens. The key to pupil self-assessment is giving the pupils a 'sufficiently clear picture of the targets that their learning is meant to attain' (pp. 9–10). When pupils have an overview of what they are learning and why they are learning it, they become 'more committed and more effective as learners' (p. 10). Thus self-assessment is, for Black and Wiliam, '*an essential component of formative assessment*' (p. 10, their emphasis).

'The evolution of effective teaching' (p. 10) is the final part of Black and Wiliam's section on the evidence about how to improve formative assessment. Here there are echoes of the framework devised by the present writer and Mary Simpson and of the work of David Perkins (see Chapter 6). Black and Wiliam argue for 'opportunities for pupils to express their understanding to be designed into any piece of teaching' (p. 11) and they focus on *dialogue*. Much has been made since the publication of *Inside the Black Box* of the place of questioning in the classroom. Teachers have been encouraged to ask more 'open' questions (questions with no single answer) as opposed to 'closed' questions. Others talk of 'fat' questions (those which lead onto in-depth discussion) rather than 'thin' or 'skinny' questions which tend to have a right answer (which is usually in the teacher's head). But recently, Wiliam has suggested that the main focus should have been on dialogue rather than questioning since in most classrooms it is the teacher who dominates the questioning process. Dialogue shifts the balance, it becomes more of a give and take and it can occur among pupils, not simply orchestrated by the teacher. It requires the engagement of *all* of the pupils, promotes 'thoughtful reflection' (p. 12) and enhances their ability to learn.

Thus, the message of *Inside the Black Box* is a powerful one, based on solid and extensive research evidence but practical in its recommendations for the classroom. The message is often distilled down to four elements:

- sharing the learning intentions
- feedback
- dialogue (and questioning)
- peer- and self-assessment.

But the underlying message is clear: formative assessment is about effective learning and teaching, deep learning and teaching for understanding. It is not a panacea but it has a firm foundation in research and in learning theory and its message has found a resonance in the work of many classroom teachers.

A Local Authority approach – Highland Council

In Highland Council, thinking skills have been at the heart of policy and practice designed to improve learning and teaching in all schools. In the early 1990s, Kevin Logan, then a Mathematics teacher in a Highland secondary school, worked with the present author to produce a postgraduate-level course aimed at teachers entitled 'Effective Learning and Teaching from a Thinking Skills Perspective'. What it lacked in the 'snappiness' of its title it made up for in clarity; the course did not attempt to persuade teachers that thinking skills was the only answer to the question of how young people learn, not least because within thinking skills as a movement, there are many different approaches (see Chapter 6). The course looked at the history of ideas, including the influence of the Scottish Enlightenment, at theories of learning, at some of the key approaches and programmes which went under the title of thinking skills, at the concept of the 'reflective professional' and at the ways in which teachers could put thinking at the heart of their pedagogy. Given the geography of the Scottish Highlands, the course had a distance learning element to it, with small groups of teachers meeting together informally, in schools, in one another's houses, in pubs, to discuss the course reading and to engage on collaborative tasks. The key was to look at how teachers could discuss ideas about pupil learning, apply some of them to their classrooms and subject both the ideas and the practice to a critique.

Gradually, over a decade or so, with the input of academics such as Professor Robert Fisher (*Teaching Children to Think*, 1990) and Professor Carol McGuinness (Activating Children's Thinking Skills: ACTS project, Northern Ireland) as well as practitioners from Highland schools, teachers met together in Inverness and Dingwall to discuss new ideas. When Assessment is for Learning emerged as a national programme in the early part of the twenty-first century, Kevin Logan was one of the first to see the connections between thinking skills and formative assessment. Now seconded as a Development Officer, he began to engage with schools through a Scottish Executive-funded project and with teachers and academics to produce a publication which was designed to help teachers move from principles to practice.

The unique elements of the Highland Council approach were, first, to see beyond the strategies of Assessment is for Learning. Thus, although WALT (Working and Learning Together), WILF (What I'm Looking For), traffic lights and jigsawing could be effective in classrooms, these were the means to an end, not an end in themselves. Formative assessment is much more than giving teachers 'handy hints' or 'tips for teaching'; it is about understanding the principles which underpin the approach. Highland Council set out these principles, derived from work within the Authority with groups of teachers who were implementing Assessment is for Learning.

Participation, dialogue, thinking and engagement were the four key principles identified. Thus, pupils actively participate in their own learning by being given feedback by the teacher or by their peers which helps them to improve the next time they attempt this aspect of learning. Peer- and self-assessment are fundamental to this process because, for it to be effective, the pupils must have internalised the criteria for success. The element of Assessment is for Learning which is often referred to as *questioning* is reconceptualised as *dialogue,* shifting the emphasis from the teacher as the locus of control and placing pupil–pupil discussion on an equal footing. For all of this to happen, the pupils must be engaged in their learning and, among other things, the exploration, sharing and negotiating of learning outcomes from the outset are key to this. However, the aim of all of this is not simply to implement Assessment is for Learning; the aim is to produce *thinking* young people. Thus the reflective professional creates a learning classroom in which thinking children learn effectively.

The Highland model puts *peer- and self-assessment* at the heart of this process. The acid test of Assessment is for Learning is whether it enables pupils to take responsibility for their own learning. 'Purposeful thinking' is the goal, and the link between Assessment is for Learning and thinking skills is set within the context of *A Curriculum for Excellence*. Not only will this approach help teachers to help their pupils to become *successful learners*, but self-directed learning will engender *confident individuals*. The collaborative elements of Assessment is for Learning, the emphasis on *dialogue* and the identification of *purposeful thinking* as a goal, are aimed at developing *effective contributors*, young people who are able to reflect on their own learning and that of their peers and who can engage in dialogue as part of their learning. And, of course, the responsibility which learners are enabled to take for their own learning, the independence and the interdependence which collaborative learning engenders, will help produce young people who are *responsible citizens*, within the classroom and in their life outside school.

Highland Council has taken a thoughtful approach to Assessment is for Learning, not least in its provision of CPD.

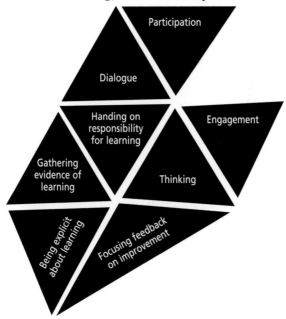

The Highland Council
Learning and Teaching CPD Reflection Framework

The Highland Council Learning and Teaching CPD Reflection Framework

Why do we need a reflection framework?
A number of national policy initiatives – A Curriculum for Excellence, Assessment is for Learning, Determined to Succeed – have, in different ways, promoted the importance of pupils becoming more actively engaged in what and how they are learning.

Pupils cannot do this by themselves. It will only happen if facilitated by their teachers. The purpose of this Framework is to stimulate, support and sustain the levels of professional reflection and self-evaluation likely to prepare them for that role.

What is the framework for?
This is not a set of course materials to be used according to a rigid formula regardless of individual school circumstances. Nor does it prescribe where schools are expected to be at some point in the future.

Sustainable change takes time and schools need to make good progress commensurate with local needs. The Framework is intended to help schools and teachers meet national policy expectations by providing opportunities to reflect on the underpinning principles and evaluate how far current practice meets them.

How does it aim to achieve this?
In the course of developing the Framework, participation, dialogue, engagement and thinking were identified as the principles most likely to support pupils in becoming actively involved in their own learning.

These principles are just as valid for teachers undertaking professional learning and, in using the Framework, participants should aim to practise them as they work together.

What does the framework provide?
Each of the six units contains resources designed for flexible use. Various short papers provide introductory reading.

PowerPoint presentations can be adapted to meet different needs: some can be divided into short sessions, each exploring a specific aspect of the main theme. The presentations are supported by handouts and discussion notes. The units also include structured activities to allow participants to explore the issues raised and supplementary materials for further reading and reflection.

How can it be used?

No two schools will have identical needs so the framework does not provide a 'one size fits all' solution. Individual elements are described opposite and this can be used to identify a suitable entry point. For example, a group of teachers looking to develop their use of assessment in the classroom could work on the first unit in Section B to help them gather together different strategies into a coherent and sustainable approach. Alternatively, a subject department with experience of formative assessment might use the second unit in Section C to think how they can meet the purposes of ACfE through their classroom work. Finally, a management team might find Section A helpful in supporting sustainable change.

The individual units have been written by Professors Brain Boyd and Robert Fisher, Mark Priestley of Stirling University, and Eric Young SEED consultant.

Section A
Managing Transformational Change

To achieve the objectives of Assessment is for Learning, A Curriculum for Excellence and Determined to Succeed, we need to stimulate a capacity for professional change and sustain the processes needed to achieve it. Isolated courses and 'cascade' approaches have not been successful in the past so this section provides school managers and practitioners with some research-based insights into what is likely to work as well as what could stifle school developments.

Unit A1
The reflective professional and the thinking child

This overview places the reflection framework in the context of the Highland Council's approach to thinking in pupils' learning and looks at the role of reflection and thinking by teachers and pupils in responding to current policy initiatives.

Unit A2
Promoting and sustaining change

This unit reviews case studies and research findings about the characteristics of change processes that are likely to prove both effective and sustainable for those involved.

Section B
Embedding Formative Assessment

This section introduces the principles of participation, dialogue, engagement and thinking which research tells us are important factors in ensuring that interactions between teachers and pupils in the classroom are likely to produce meaningful learning experiences for all involved.

Unit B1
Embedding formative assessment:
So what are the pupils doing?

This unit explores the principles and practice of formative assessment and emphasises the role of pupil peer- and self-assessment in ensuring its effectiveness in the classroom.

Unit B2
Making thinking explicit

This unit looks at the role of thinking by pupils as an essential element in helping them to become more involved in their own learning and so take greater responsibility for it.

Section C
Extending Formative Assessment

In these units, the principles and practice discussed in Section A are developed to guide how schools might engage with personal learning planning and local moderation and with A Curriculum for Excellence.

Unit C1
Around the Assessment is for Learning triangle

Assessment AS learning (personal learning planning) and OF learning (local moderation) depend on pupils and teachers who are able to inform their judgements about what needs to be done next with the evidence of progress they have gathered. This unit investigates how teaching focused on providing pupils with opportunities to assess themselves can be developed to support the other aspects of AifL.

Unit C2
Engaging purposes, principles and practice

In setting out its purposes and the principles of curriculum design, A Curriculum for Excellence has signalled a shift from a curriculum focused on delivering subject-based outcomes to one which also aims to help all children and young people achieve their personal potential and learn how to play an active part in the community around them. This unit examines how the classroom practices associated with AifL can help teachers meet these objectives.

The Highland Council Learning and Teaching CPD Reflection Framework

Building on the CPD programme, Highland has sought to embed and extend formative assessment within its schools. It won funding from the then Scottish Executive Education Department's Future Learning and Teaching (FLaT) programme to enable three 'clusters' of schools to develop Assessment is for Learning. At the time of writing, the project is ongoing but already the 'Highland model' is attracting attention across Scotland and beyond. It has steadfastly refused to see Assessment is for Learning merely as a set of activities to be introduced into the classroom. It has challenged the complacent attitude which sometimes is articulated in the phrases 'It's just good teaching' or 'I've been doing this for years', which are sometimes heard when formative assessment is discussed. Rather it has set out to engage teachers in a professional discussion about the *why* of formative assessment as well as giving them access to strategies which can be used in the classroom. And, at all stages, it has tried to make the connections between Assessment is for Learning and A Curriculum for Excellence.

Embedding
A Curriculum for Excellence
in the Classroom

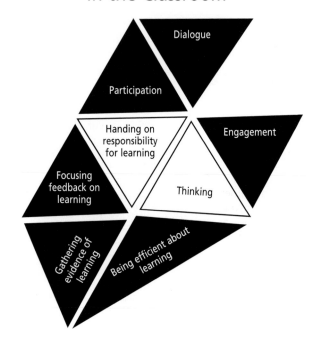

A Route to Engagement
This guide builds upon the Highland Council Reflection
Framework and the recent programme of CPD
activities to promote continuing professional development
around helping pupils take greater responsibility for
their own learning.

www.hvlc.org.uk/ace/aifl/

Reflective Professionals and Thinking Children

Fostering the CfE capacities through the principles and practice of formative assessment

Introduction

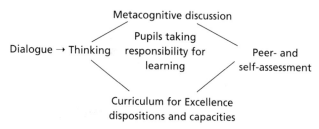

The diagram above is the central section of the model of the principles and practice of formative assessment as explored in the Highland Council Learning and Teaching CPD Reflection Framework. More recent Highland CPD activities have been focussed on further developing those aspects of the framework as they relate to Curriculum for Excellence and this 'road map' is designed to guide you through the additional support materials now available to further explore the Highland model and so complement continuing work on the framework. Paul Black's paper 'Full Marks for Feedback' suggests a number of ways in which dialogue and self-assessment by pupils can be carried forward and helps to confirm the validity of the Highland approach.

Reading   Paul Black: Full marks for feedback

A Exploring the principles of formative assessment

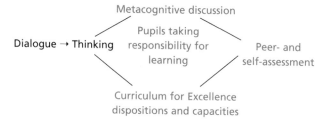

In the Highland model, the four principles underpinning formative assessment are Participation, Dialogue, Engagement and Thinking. In exploring these principles further, we have concentrated on the practical implications of developing thinking through effective dialogue in the classroom. In focusing on this, we are beginning to explore what is involved in improving pupils' capacity to learn and the role of dialogue and self-assessment in developing how we optimise how we understand and use formative assessment.

Reading   Highland CPD Reflection
                                 Framework unit B1
Engagement activity   Assessing dialogue

B Developing formative assessment practices

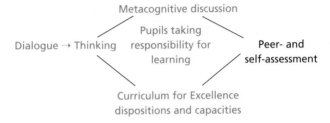

Peer and self-assessment has become an important part of the development work undertaken by teachers in Highland schools over the past year. We now have a body of case studies describing the experiences of teachers and pupils at all stages and initial indications suggest that peer- and self-assessment offer significant opportunities for real improvement even in upper secondary where formative assessment is often regarded with some caution.

Reading   Unit B1 (Sessions 3 and 4),
                                 Highland peer- and self-
                                 assessment case studies
Engagement activity   Peer- and self-assessment

C Creating autonomous learners

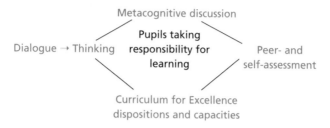

The Highland Council Reflection Framework was always about using the principles and practice of formative assessment as the practical basis upon which the purposes of Curriculum for Excellence could be achieved. If children and young people learn how to become more involved in their own learning and so take greater personal responsibility for it, then they will be well on the way to displaying the capacities of successful learners, confident individuals, responsible citizens and effective contributors. Recent CPD work has allowed us to focus attention on both affective and cognitive aspects of the dispositions children and young people need to bring to their learning.

1 Affective aspects
Reading — Unit C1 (Session 2), Learning Dispositions and Personal Learning Planning, Guidance on writing learning logs
Engagement activity — Words of Praise, Exploring learning logs
2 Cognitive aspects
Reading — Unit B2, Thinking to Learn, Tools for Learning (Robert Fisher)
Engagement activity — Auditing thinking and learning.

Embedding a Curriculum for Excellence in the Classroom

The original Highland model was designed to show that the principles and practice of formative assessment can offer an effective and rigorous way to meet the needs of a Curriculum for Excellence. From the start, the central theme of the model was the role of teachers in helping pupils to take greater responsibility for their own learning. The 2007–8 programme of CPD activities has begun to explore in more detail the essential elements of this role. The modified model below highlights the focus of recent activities. In addressing these aspects of classroom practice, we can begin to develop a meaningful way of engaging with both the values, purposes and principles of a Curriculum for Excellence and the new self-evaluation framework of How Good is our School: the journey to excellence.

P
R
I
N
C
I
P
L
E
S

Participation

Dialogue ⟶ Thinking

Engagement

Metacognitive
discussion

**Pupils taking
responsibility for
learning**

Affective aspects:
Learning dispositions
Feedback
Personal learning
Planning

Cognitive aspects:
Critical thinking
Creative thinking
Information processing

ACfE
dispositions and capacities
(critical and creative thinkers)

**Peer- & self-
assessment**

Being explicit
about learning

P
R
A   C
      T
      I   C
      E

Gathering
evidence
of learning

Focusing
feedback on
improvement

Unlocking formative assessment

One of the most influential disseminators of the formative assessment message has been Shirley Clarke. Her books on how to put into practice the principles of formative assessment in the primary classroom have been best sellers and she is in demand as a CPD facilitator. *Unlocking Formative Assessment* (2006) is typical of her books. It begins with a reference to *Inside the Black Box,* reminding the reader that the origin of the current interest in formative assessment was the literature review carried out by the two academics from the Kings College, London.

The bulk of the book, derived in no small part from her successful work with teachers on in-service courses and in research projects, is made up of practical strategies and solutions, in a 'down to earth and direct' attempt to 'give teachers the "how to" information they really need'. The book is full of examples of approaches and formats used by teachers and schools, children's writing and how teachers respond to it, suggestions for INSET activities and a helpful set of references for further reading. In short, used in a CPD context, rather than as a manual or a set of 'tips-for-teachers', this book is helpful.

The challenge is for school and curriculum leaders to use books like Shirley Clarke's in ways which open up discussion. She deals with difficult issues, including *self-esteem* and *praise*, where conventional thinking has been challenged in recent years (see Chapter 10). She also tries to distil the research evidence in a way which makes it accessible to teachers – again a helpful approach given the arcane language and style in which much academic research is couched.

The challenge for Scottish teachers, now that reading has been established as a legitimate aspect of CPD, is to engage with research in ways which empower them to take a critical stance when another new initiative comes along. The view that teachers cannot, or are unwilling to, engage with theory and research, is patronising. The notion that they have to have others simplify research findings for them is also insulting. What is helpful is to have a range of options, from the original research reports to 'how to' books like Shirley Clarke's. The common thread is CPD, allowing time and opportunity for teachers to engage with new ideas, individually or with colleagues.

Principles of the formative classroom

The formative classroom may well be a misnomer, just as formative assessment does not wholly describe the initiative which has become known as Assessment is for Learning (AifL). It would be hard to conceive of how assessment could exist independently of learning and teaching. But, in Scotland, in the run up to the elections to the Scottish Parliament, schools were encouraged to become 'AifL schools' by 2007. This was later softened a little to 'be on the way to becoming an AifL school' by 2007 (the year of the election). So, in this context, the following could be said to be the principles of the formative classroom:

- *Feedback* Assessment in the past was too often simply a *post hoc* verdict on pupils' performance; it had little impact on their future learning. In the formative classroom, feedback will rarely, if ever, be in the form of marks or grades; it will be given not just by the teacher but by the learner her/himself or by peers. Its principal purpose will be to enable the learner to be more successful next time.
- *Dialogue* In traditional classrooms, as Flanders (1970) pointed out (Chapter 1), most of the talk which went on was teacher-talk and most of that was questioning and giving instructions. Often the answer the child gave to the teacher's (normally closed) question was the end, rather than the beginning, of a dialogue. Now, in the formative classroom, dialogue is at the heart of learning. Pupils, given the rationale for dialogue and the skills and strategies to engage in it profitably, learn to ask as well as answer questions, and initiate discussion, with peers and with the teacher.
- *Pupils taking responsibility for their own learning* Too often the demands on teachers in the classroom to 'get through the curriculum/syllabus' or to prepare pupils for the test or exam mean that didactic teaching dominates. Pace of learning is often dictated by external pressures rather than by the understanding of the learners. Deep learning is sacrificed in the face of demands for recall and superficial regurgitation of knowledge. In the formative classroom, pupils make decisions, reflect on their own and others' learning and, through dialogue with fellow pupils and with the teacher, become more autonomous learners.

POINTS FOR REFLECTION

1 Why do you think Assessment is for Learning has made such an impact on Scottish classrooms in a relatively short period of time?

2 Highland Council has tried to link AifL to thinking skills and to move from principles to practice. What is your view of their approach?

3 What are your views of the principles of *the formative classroom?*

4 The thinking classroom

 If the teacher is also learning, teaching takes on a new quality.
Jerome Bruner, *The Process of Education*

Preamble

The term 'thinking skills' has been around in education for a generation or more. It has sound theoretical and empirical foundations and it has some big hitters in the educational community promoting its benefits. The main argument has been whether children and young people should be taught thinking skills in isolation, as a separate component in the curriculum, or whether thinking skills should be *infused* into every subject. And, of course, there are those who argue for a third way, with a dedicated course on thinking skills, backed up by strategies and approaches within individual subjects.

In this chapter we consider the historical antecedents of today's thinking skills programmes and philosophies, looking at the work of major international thinkers, including Bruner and Bloom, Vygotsky and Feuerstein, Lipman and De Bono and, closer to home, Nisbet and Entwistle. Margaret Kirkwood (2005) has written in some depth on the work of David Perkins from Harvard and his Teaching for Understanding approach. This chapter touches on the key elements of Perkins' work and his most recent idea, whole-game learning. We look at key strategies associated with thinking skills, from mind mapping (Buzan, 1993) to thinking hats (De Bono, 1973) and at some case studies of classrooms, schools and local authorities which are pioneering the development of thinking in young people.

Thinking skills: fostering independent learning?

There is something inherently paradoxical about the concept of thinking skills. After all, didn't Descartes argue conclusively that *cogito ergo sum?* If thinking defines us as human, if it is natural and ubiquitous, how can it be seen as a set of 'skills'? Robert Fisher (1990) has posed the question 'what is thinking?' and cites Matthew Lipman's analogy of the car mechanic who might have the same tools as the car owner but has, in addition, the insight to 'organise and sequence the use of the tools to repair the engine' (Fisher, 1990, p. x). Fisher argues that higher-order thinking skills can, and should, be taught, and that, while thinking skills can be organised into taxonomies, they are not to be seen as separate and distinct. Thus, while it is possible to list characteristics of *creative* or *critical* thinkers, we must give learners the insights and strategies to become proficient in both. Nor is thinking to be seen as purely cognitive or cerebral; the emotions are an integral part of thinking. Indeed, Fisher suggests that 'It is the linking of reason with emotion that provides the prime motivation for learning, and for the development of intelligence' (p. x). Later in the book, he cites Vygotsky who postulated that 'all psychological processes are the result of social and cultural interaction' (p. 7). Importantly for teachers, Vygotsky's belief is that 'it is through the use of language that children take control of their thinking ...' (p. 7). Vygotsky's famous dictum 'what the child can do in co-operation [with others] today, he will do alone tomorrow' (p. 7) clearly suggests that collaborative learning is not simply an end in itself; it is a step along the way towards independent learning. Thus, as we shall see in Chapter 9, collaborative learning is important in developing the capacity for thinking in individual learners.

Matthew Lipman (2003), writing from a philosophical perspective, considers what 'Schooling without Thinking' looks like. He describes 'a loss of curiosity and imagination' (p. 12) and suggests when this phenomenon occurs in classrooms some teachers will 'condemn the child's background' (p. 12). He suggest that the child's pre-school world is often extraordinary; 'the uncanniness is evocative; it draws speech out of the child' (p. 13). He is critical of the 'completely structured environment' (p. 13) of many elementary schools. The language of the classroom has lost the richness of the home and the community (however disadvantaged). His accusation that 'schooling provides few natural incentives to thinking' (p. 13) seems harsh to the Scottish reader, since early years education, rightly, enjoys a high reputation; but we know what he means. Routine, it has been argued, is the enemy of creativity, and, for many young children, formal education is the beginning of the end of their natural inclination to be learners. Lipman does not blame teachers for this; rather it is the formality of the curriculum, the tyranny of assessment regimes and the drive for accountability to be found in advanced industrial countries across the world in the late twentieth and early twenty-first centuries.

Thinking skills is no passing fad, some educational flibbertigibbet, with little theoretical underpinning. We have noted the links with Vygotsky, and Furth and Wachs have argued that thinking skills represent 'Piaget's Theory in Practice'. In their book *Thinking Goes to School* (1974), they attempt to describe 'a school for thinking' based on their work in Charleston, West Virginia, in the early 1970s. The two writers had five objectives in their work with the school, namely to develop:

- the habit of creative, independent thinking
- a positive self image in the children
- attitudes to social cooperation and moral responsibility
- a knowledge and appreciation of persons, things and events in the environment
- competence in the basic skill areas of reading, writing and arithmetic.

(p. 5)

It must be said that, nearly four decades on, these objectives are not dissimilar from those of most advanced industrial countries, including Scotland. Part of their approach also involved the creation of 'a Thinking School Classroom' and they list a number of characteristics of such a classroom:

1 The activity of thinking is worthwhile in itself
2 Structured activities to enhance the child's developing intelligence
3 Activities designed to challenge the child's thinking but not too difficult so as to invite failure

4 The child is involved in, and focuses his attention on, the activity and not on the teacher as ... the source of knowledge

5 Activities are performed by each individual child within a group of peers with whom he relates socially and cooperates

6 The teacher provides a model of the thinking person for the children.

(pp. 45–46)

The bulk of Furth and Wachs' book is taken up with thinking games, some 160 of them, which were used to develop children's thinking. The authors, in their final chapter, lament the fact that their evidence for the success of this approach is 'only qualitative' and cite lack of funding for the project's premature end and, therefore, lack of quantitative evidence. They make the point that, when schools set out to become thinking schools, they must 'resist the unreasonable pressure for quick performance results' (p. 299). They add that 'the development of the thinking child will take time' (p. 299) and point out that schools (in the 1970s) were 'under pain of turning out result after result that may have statistical but no psychological significance' (p. 299).

Four decades later, similar sentiments are often heard from teachers and headteachers who feel under pressure to improve results, as measured by tests and examinations. If the secondary school's exam results are deemed unsatisfactory, subject departments are visited in September by a member of the senior management team to discuss 'relative ratings' – statistics designed to compare the school, and each department within it, with 'comparators', i.e. schools deemed to be similar. Any improvement has to be made between September and May of the following year, when the next cohorts of pupils sit their exams. Eight months seems a short time for the kinds of improvements often demanded of teachers. If the development of the thinking child does, in fact, take time then the process needs to begin in early years education and the criteria by which progress is measured need to be more sophisticated than the current model of external exam.

In Scotland, *A Curriculum for Excellence* offers a unique opportunity for the education system of a whole country, catering for pupils from age 3 to 18, to create this time and to be bold enough to take a long-term view of the educational process. It was Eliot Eisner (1985) who argued that education is not a preparation for exams but a preparation for life. If we believe this, what are the kinds of characteristics we wish to develop in our young people and how can we do this without compromising their chances of success in a competitive world?

Habits of mind

The American academic Art Costa has identified a number of 'dispositions' or 'habits of mind' which can help human beings behave intelligently when confronted by problems. He does not claim that his list of 16 is exhaustive or even that they are original. He acknowledges his indebtedness to the work of other thinkers such as Feuerstein, Perkins, Sternberg, Ennis and Goleman. Costa suggests that teachers can make these habits of mind explicit to learners and suggests that in so doing they can introduce the learners to more productive patterns of behaviour, inculcating in them a tendency to employ these habits of mind in learning contexts and to have the capacity to persevere when problems arise by reflecting on their performances.

Costa has outlined the 16 *habits of mind* on his website, **www.habitsofmind.org**; 12 of them are described below:

Persisting

Many learners lack stickability in the face of difficulty. Persistence comes with having a range of strategies and having the confidence to re-group when things are going wrong.

Listening to others – with understanding and empathy

Covey (1989) has observed that highly effective people spend a huge amount of time listening – a key social skill as well as one which supports learning. Schools rarely 'teach' listening skills, assuming that pupils have them naturally. A good listener respects the views of the other person and wants to understand, if not necessarily agree with, her views.

Metacognition

It would help if young people were introduced in school not simply to what they have to learn but to how they can learn. This requires time, and is put at risk if the curriculum is all about coverage and dictated by examinations. Teachers can help also by asking 'How did you solve that problem? What strategies did you use?' and 'What was going on in your head when you were working on that problem?'

Striving for precision

The image of the traditional craftsperson, labouring tirelessly on tasks in which s/he takes pride is useful here. Working and re-working, drafting and re-drafting is not routine or mundane work. It requires reflection, an understanding of the criteria for success and an intrinsic desire to do well.

Applying past knowledge to new situations

Learning from experience is part of the human condition. It has helped the species survive and evolve. Teachers can help not only by building on past knowledge but by drawing attention to strategies used in the past to solve similar problems. If pupils do not intuitively apply previous knowledge or strategies then teachers can help direct their attention.

Thinking and communicating with clarity and precision

Costa argues, as others have done before him, that 'Language and thinking are closely entwined' (p. 12). Therefore, the teacher must strive to enrich 'the complexity and specificity of language' in the learners. Thus, the importance of defining terms, giving explanations, making comparisons and basing opinions on evidence is what the teacher should emphasise.

Gathering data through all senses

The brain gathers its data through the senses. In everyday life, we can go through the day oblivious to the 'textures, rhythms, patterns, sounds and colours' around us. Thus, learning should focus *all* of the senses, not simply those which support reading and writing. Howard Gardner's *multiple intelligences* (1983) are an indication of the importance for all pupils of seeing learning as a multi-faceted, multi-sensory process.

Creating, imagining and innovating

Costa argues that 'all human beings have the capacity to generate novel, original, clever or ingenious products, solutions and techniques – if that capacity is developed' (p. 13). He refers to David Perkins (1995) who suggested that creative people 'frequently push the boundaries of their perceived limits'. Creative people are not 'just born that way'; they work hard at it and they persevere.

Taking responsible risks

In Scotland, a member of HMIE said at the Conference of Headteachers in South Lanarkshire (2005) that teachers should 'take risks without being reckless'. Costa talks of 'flexible people ... willing to accept confusion, uncertainty and the higher risk of failure' associated with risk-taking. They need to know, too, when not to take a risk, when to weigh the evidence and make a considered judgement. The French footballer Thierry Henry is credited with the saying 'I hate to lose, but I'm not afraid to fail', which neatly sums up this habit of mind.

Finding humour

A sense of humour is a uniquely human characteristic. Laughter has all sorts of positive effects on our psychological and physiological functions. We know too that wit and repartee demand a quick mind, making connection, seeing absurdity, making analogies. The use of humour is a feature in the classrooms of all successful teachers. It is also high on the list of attributes identified by pupils in successful teachers. Thus, humour is not simply an accidental by-product of learning; it is an integral part of it.

Thinking interdependently

Vygotsky (1978) was the educational theorist who most thoroughly explored the links between learning and social interaction. Costa argues that pupils need to learn to work in groups (see Chapter 9). They need to learn how to justify ideas and test their theories on others; to be willing to accept feedback and criticism from a 'critical friend'. Listening, consensus-seeking, as well as compassion, empathy and leadership, can all be developed through interdependent learning.

Learning continuously

Costa quotes Enstein: 'Insanity is continuing to do the same thing over and over and expecting different results' (p. 16). Continuing learning, striving for improvement, modifying strategies and pursuing deep learning is what successful learners do. Too often the school curriculum fragments learning, chunks it up into short episodes and expects the learners to be passive recipients. Learning continuously involves being humble about what we don't know and being willing to find out.

For Costa, habits of mind 'transcend all subject matters commonly taught in schools' (p. 18). If the aim of education is to prepare pupils for life rather than simply for exams, then the *content* of education may be less important than the skills and dispositions which young people acquire throughout their schooling. Thus by making these habits of mind explicit and by developing them in every area of the curriculum, Costa believes that young people will become successful, life-long learners. He quotes Aristotle to emphasise this point:

> We are what we repeatedly do. Excellence, then, is not an act but a habit.

Making thinking explicit

In the past, it was not uncommon for pupils to be in the dark about why they were learning what the teacher had asked them to do. Stories to illustrate this phenomenon abound. The present author visited an S2 Maths class in the early 1990s as part of a research project. The following conversation, initiated by the researcher, ensued:

'What are you doing?'
'A booklet.'
'Which booklet?'
At this point the pupil had to turn to the front cover to check.
'*Whole Numbers.*'
'What happens when you finish this booklet?'

'I take it to the teacher and he marks it.'

'And then what?'

'I do another booklet.'

'Which one?'

'I don't know. The teacher will decide.'

Finally, the researcher asked:

'Is there anyone else in the class at the moment doing the booklet on *Whole Numbers*?'

'I don't know.'

In fact, there were at least three other pupils doing the booklet on *Whole Numbers,* but in this individualised learning approach, promoted vigorously by HMI at the time, there was little opportunity for what Costa calls 'interdependent learning'. Indeed, not only did the pupil have little idea of what she was doing or why she was doing it, there was no input from her on *how* she was learning. There was no discussion to enable her to embed her learning, no sharing of insights among learners and no ownership by the pupils of the learning process. In this, albeit extreme, example very little was made explicit.

Since the late 1990s, the emphasis has shifted, partially as a result of the impact of *Inside the Black Box* (see Chapter 3), to sharing the learning goals with the pupils at the outset of the lesson or sequence of lessons. The basis of this change is the research evidence which shows that pupils learn more effectively if they are aware of the 'big picture', or, as David Perkins puts it, they are participating in *whole-game learning.* His contention is that many pupils simply do not understand the purpose of the learning they are being asked to do. He uses the analogy of the baseball game – for the Scottish reader, football might be more relevant. When young children are learning to play a game, such as football, they watch it, they play 'junior versions' of it, like two- or three- or five-a-side. They play with jackets for goalposts; they play 'headers', 'shooty-in', penalties, and so on. They would quickly be turned off, argues Perkins, if all they got to do was endlessly practise individual skills, with no knowledge of how these fitted into the whole game and with no opportunity to play the game itself. He extends the analogy by saying that the only way in which we can judge if pupils have truly *understood* what they are learning is if they can *play away from home,* applying their learning in new and unfamiliar contexts. This is the antithesis of what happens with exams, where teachers spend inordinate amounts of time getting pupils to do 'past papers', second-guessing what might come up in the examination itself and drilling the pupils in the kinds of answers they might give. For David Perkins (1995), there are 13 steps a teacher can take to create a thinking classroom:

Provoke genuine discussion

The key word here is *genuine*. Historically, teachers manipulated class discussions, asking all the questions, leading the pupils to a destination the teacher had already mapped out. What we need to try to do, argues Perkins, is organise the learning through *generative topics*, rich and engaging, drawing often on more than one discipline, which encourage genuine discussion where pupils are actively engaged.

The present writer, in his youth, was not immune from the practice of asking all the questions, as the following exchange somewhat embarrassingly shows. The year is 1977, it is the first lesson with a newly arrived S1 class and it is based on a poem by Stephen Spender entitled 'My Parents'. The poem has been read and the teacher is trying to elucidate its meaning by the judicious use of questions, before setting the pupils some tasks:
Did anyone else find anything difficult in the poem? *What's the meaning of the word lithe? (Maria)* Yes. I thought someone might ask that. Have a look at the third verse, beginning of the first line, it says, talking about the boys who were making a fool of him. (Quote: 'They were lithe, they sprang out behind hedges/ Like dogs to bark at my world.') Has anyone ever seen it before? No. Well, what happens when you come across a word in a book that you've never seen before? How can you figure out what it means without looking it up in a dictionary? How could you guess what it means? *Read it and see how it fits in with the other words? (Lawrie)* Yes. (Teacher repeats the pupil's answer.) How ... Lithe? How could you guess it? Look for a clue in the word 'spring'. *Wild?* Yes, it does mean a wee bit wild. *Cunning?* Yes, it's got ideas of cunning in it as well. *Lively?* Yes, that's getting closer. *Shy?* Yes, right. Now let me give you a hint. You could talk about a ... cheetah, or a

panther, or something like that, being lithe ... springing ... right? *Stealthy* O.K. Now try and think of HOW it springs. *Energetic? Fast?* Yes. (Teacher repeats the answers.) *Pounces?* Yes. Now let's say that I thought Peter Latchford is the best goalie in Scotland because he is very lithe – *Agile?* Yes. That's it.

(Brian Boyd, *Beginning Group Work in S1*, 1979)

Let learners ask (and answer) questions

Shifting the balance of questioning from the teacher to the learner is at the heart of cooperative learning (see Chapter 9). Black and Wiliam (1998) have suggested that the average 'wait time' allowed by teachers after a question is asked is 0.9 seconds, after which they either re-phrase the question or identify a pupil to answer, often to his great consternation if he does not know the answer.

Display the conduct of a thinker

Teachers are thinkers, and learners, too. It is OK for a teacher to say, 'I don't know the answer to that question. Let me think. How would we find that out?' It is equally important that the teacher embeds thinking in the ongoing work of the class, saying to the class 'I have a question to ask and I want you to take 30 seconds "think time" with your partner and I'll take some answers.' In this one sentence, the teacher shows that thinking is valued, that it can be a collaborative activity, that it takes time and that there can be more than one answer to a question posed by the teacher. The next step is for pupils to ask one another questions, the pre-requisite being that they know the kinds of questions they are asking and that they have at least some of the answers.

Give thinking time

Thinking time is important. It is not a waste of time, nor is it off-task behaviour. Nor does it conflict with the HMIE concept of 'pace of learning'. In fact, it is exactly what is meant by the principle of *depth*, introduced by *A Curriculum for Excellence*.

However, given the current pressure on teachers to get through the curriculum, 'coverage' (Boyd and Simpson, 2000) becomes the driver, and teachers are wary of giving up time for thinking. A further pressure on teachers is what they see as an HMIE emphasis on 'evidence' when they come to inspect schools. Thus, if thinking does not yield as much writing as before, teachers may be reluctant to engage in it. The paradox, of course, is that if deep learning (Entwistle, 2000) is to be the aim of *A Curriculum for Excellence,* thinking cannot be an optional extra.

Use the language of thinking

Perkins argues that teachers and pupils should use the language of thinking, in the same way as they are expected to use the language of science, or literary criticism, or historical analysis. In the Scottish context, it is not generally known that the 5–14 curriculum, implemented in the late 1980s, placed a strong emphasis on thinking in the Rationale sections of the Guidelines documents. Thus, when the English Language document suggested that:

> Schools should provide structured and stimulating opportunities to use language with increasing precision in contexts appropriate to the needs of individuals and the world in which they live. Providing such opportunities will involve the following:
> **Thinking:** for example, speculating; hypothesizing; discovering; reflecting; generalising; synthesizing; evaluating.
> (Scottish Consultative Council on the Curriculum, 1980, p. 3)

Perkins would argue that the terminology should be used as well as the strategies to promote these types of thinking.

Use (more) open-ended questions

The issue of open or open-ended questions has become prominent since the publication of *Inside the Black Box.* Black and Wiliam argued that, in too many classrooms, too many of the questions were 'closed', i.e. they had only one *right* answer (normally the one in the teacher's head). However, the injunction to use more open questions was often misunderstood, so much so that Dylan Wiliam later made it clear that the open/closed distinction could be misleading. For example, is the question 'What colour is the sky?' an open or a closed question? Well if you live in the Caribbean it might be closed, the answer being 'Blue'. In other countries, there would be many different answers; indeed, the question itself may be meaningless. Some have talked of 'thin' and 'fat' questions, questions which either close off or open up a dialogue. The key is to be aware, as a teacher or a learner, of the different kinds of questions, and to use a better balance than previously.

Use small-group/paired learning

Chapter 9 looks at the cooperative classroom in some detail. For Perkins, understanding is the key, and understanding, as Vygotsky suggests, comes when human beings interact socially, discussing ideas and making sense of the world. Robin Alexander's *Towards Dialogic Teaching* (2004, 2006) offers a structured approach to giving pupils, from a very young age, the skills for working in groups and a rationale for learning in this way.

Teach pupils some simple thinking strategies

There are lots of thinking strategies around. The aim of these strategies is to enable pupils to be problem solvers and decision makers. Perkins would argue that these, and many other, strategies should be make available to the pupils so that they have a repertoire at their finger tips and can use them when they encounter difficulties in their learning.

Unveil thinking through questions

The role of questioning in the learning process is well known, at a 'common-sense' and at a theoretical level. The inquisitive child, the parent who answers questions patiently and fully, the discussion which accompanies reading from an early age, are all associated with good learning foundations. For Perkins, it is through thoughtful questioning that teachers can unveil the pupil's thinking. The aim is not to get the 'right' answer, necessarily; rather it is to help the learner make explicit her/his thinking processes so that they can be applied in similar, and in new, circumstances.

Encourage metacognition

Metacognition has become something of a Holy Grail in recent years. Perkins' focus on *understanding* is designed to promote deep rather than surface learning. Learning *how* rather than simply *what* has been a consistent theme of Tony Buzan's work for more than three decades. Equipping learners with the right attitudes, as well as giving them a wide range of strategies for learning, must be the aim of every teacher.

Allow pupils to 'perform' their learning

Perkins' notion of 'understanding performances' is about as far as we can get from the conventional exam. The latter involves preparing learners for the known, the predictable, by rehearsing previous exam papers. The timed element of the exam usually ensures that pupils have to write very quickly, so time for reflection, for consideration of the nuances of exam questions and for demonstrating deep understanding, is at a premium. Not only that, since the exam tends to come at the end of the course, if any misunderstandings are revealed, it is often too late to remedy them. Performances of understanding should take place throughout the learning process and should involve a range of approaches – from debates to presentations, from mock trials to wall displays – other than traditional tests or exams.

Link thinking to values

'It's good to talk.' So says the advert for a well-known telephone company. Well, it's also 'good to think'. We should promote thinking as a worthwhile activity. Many pupils, from a very early stage of schooling, come to believe that anything which does not involve reading or writing is not actually *work*. And yet Carol McGuinness (1999) is at pains to point out that thinking is 'effortful', but ultimately worthwhile. If thinking really is worth doing, we should explain its benefits to the pupils.

Find opportunities for thinking

The 10–14 Report (Consultative Committee on the Curriculum, 1986) suggested that 'the classroom crackles with subliminal signals'. Perkins suggests that teachers should reconsider their curricula and look for opportunities to inject thinking into their lessons. This chimes with his view that sometimes we teach things in ways which are too 'tame', often because of pressures of tests and examinations. He advocates that we should 'wild the tame' and find new approaches to old subject matter. If we can present old knowledge in new ways, incorporating approaches which challenge the learners to think rather than absorb knowledge, not only will the learning be more motivational but the understanding will be at a deeper level.

Principles of the thinking classroom

Given that thinking skills have been promoted for so long in education and that, over the years, a number of manifestations have emerged, is it possible to extract key underlying principles which might help teachers in classrooms help their pupils to become better thinkers and learners? Would these same principles help teachers make sense of the next programme or approach which is recommended to them? How can teachers become more confident about subjecting new ideas to a critique?

- *Metacognition* is at the heart of all thinking skills approaches and programmes. The aim is to enable learners to be knowledgeable about themselves as learners, to reflect on how they are successful and to select new strategies when they hit problems. A strategy becomes truly metacognitive when the learner is aware of *why* it is successful. Thus, the more self-knowledge learners have, the more access they have to a range of learning strategies and the more they understand about the learning process itself (including related concepts, such as intelligence), the more likely they are to be flexible, adaptable learners.
- *Understanding* Metacognition is not an end in itself. The end is *understanding*, or 'deep' learning, which will enable young people to apply principles to new and unanticipated contexts. Pupils should be given opportunities to perform their understanding as part of their ongoing learning activities (not just in the end-of-section test). The ability to apply different kinds of thinking to the solution of real problems is one way to characterise *the thinking classroom*.

- *Self-knowledge and the affective domain*
  Learning, as Carla Hannaford (1995) has argued, does not only take place inside your head. The emotions, the brain itself and the body, all play a part. The more that pupils know about this complex process and, for example, how intelligence relates to learning (see Chapter 10), the better equipped they will be when they encounter difficulties with learning. The concept of emotional intelligence has been contested since Daniel Goleman popularised it in 1996, but the elements which are included in the definition – empathy, self-control, resilience, etc. – remain important aspects of the learning process which teachers can help pupils to come to understand more fully.

POINTS FOR REFLECTION

1. Do schools, at present, foster thinking and independent learning?

2. What do you think of the advice which Costa and Perkins offer to teachers?

3. What are your views of the principles of *the learning classroom*?

5 The motivated classroom

> 'And if anyone knows anything about anything' said Bear to himself, 'it's Owl, who knows something about something,' he said, 'or my name's not Winnie-the-Pooh,' he said. 'Which it is,' he added. 'So, there you are.'
>
> **A. A. Milne, *Winnie the Pooh***

Preamble

The perennial problem of pupil motivation has been the subject of debate from the staffroom to the groves of academe. There are theories of motivation and there is the constant battle to try to motivate learners who appear to have no internal motivation for what teachers want them to learn. Perspectives on the issue vary: David Perkins (1995) suggests that much of what we teach young people is irrelevant and too 'tame' and he suggests that we move away from a model which values 'knowing a lot' to one which focuses on *understanding*. He suggests that we should 'wild the tame' and make our topics more 'generative'. Black and Wiliam (1998) emphasise the need for learners to know the 'big picture'; others emphasise active learning, collaborative approaches and enterprising cultures. But how do we reach those young people who become disengaged? What can teachers do to create a motivated classroom?

Recently, Alan McLean (2003, 2008) has written persuasively about the issue, adding to a body of work from educationists as diverse as Noel Entwistle and Daniel Goleman. There are many theories of motivation in psychology textbooks, and there has been research into how good teachers motivate learners, from the pupil perspective (Rudduck *et al.*, 1996; Boyd and Lawson, 2004) and from a teacher's perspective (Brown and McIntyre, 1993). A related concept currently being given attention in

Scotland is that of *confidence*; Carole Craig, having written *The Scots' Crisis of Confidence* (2003) and established the Centre for Confidence and Wellbeing in Glasgow with Government support, has produced an important new book, *Creating Confidence: A Handbook for Professionals Working With Young People* (2007). Given that one of the four purposes of *A Curriculum for Excellence* is 'confident individuals' the questions have to be asked: What do we mean by confidence? Is there a crisis within Scottish society? Is confidence linked to motivation to learn?

In this chapter we look both at theory and at practice. Good teachers, as we know from our experience, from popular literature and from research, inspire learners. How do they do it? Are their skills transferable? If the problem of motivating boys seems to be more acute than that of girls, what are the causes and what are some of the solutions? Theories, research evidence and the work of real teachers are considered and some principles identified.

Theories of motivation

Writing in 1987, Noel Entwistle of Edinburgh University reviewed some of the historical evidence from research into motivation in learning. He began with the early behaviourists who saw motivation as a set of forces, either internal or external. Externally, these could be manipulated by re-inforcement or reward of positive behaviours. Internal 'drivers' such as hunger or fear could be used with animals, while with humans these would be more likely to be psychological needs. Maslow (1970) posited his 'hierarchy of needs', arguing that the lower-order needs had to be satisfied before the higher-order needs could be addressed.

Entwistle (1987) argued that, while many of the practices of the behaviourists have fallen into disuse, some of the principles remain sound. Rewards and compliments are still a part of most child-rearing manuals. Entwistle cited the Hungarian Kozeki (1985) who identified three 'domains of reward – affective, cognitive and moral' (p. 130). Basing his theory on a study involving interviews with more than 1,000 children and parents, Kozeki found that most parents come to rely on only one domain. Teachers, similarly, varied in their approaches. He argued that children develop preferences depending on their early experiences and these become 'sets of motives'; Kozeki identified, through his interviews with the young people, three sub-divisions of each of the three domains:

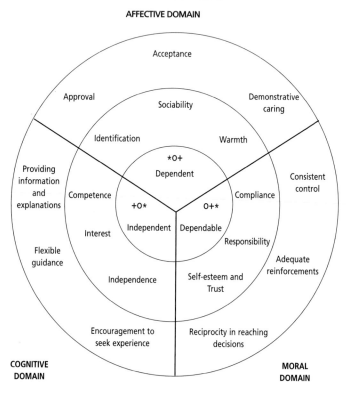

AFFECTIVE DOMAIN

Acceptance

Approval

Sociability

Demonstrative caring

Identification

Warmth

*O+

Dependent

Providing information and explanations

Competence

Consistent control

Compliance

+O*

O+*

Independent | Dependable

Interest

Responsibility

Flexible guidance

Independence

Self-esteem and Trust

Adequate reinforcements

Encouragement to seek experience

Reciprocity in reaching decisions

COGNITIVE DOMAIN

MORAL DOMAIN

Key:
Outer circle: behaviour of parents or teachers;
Inner circle: motives;
Centre: most successful motivational styles.

Kozeki suggested that young people developed *motivational styles* which were combinations of elements from domains. Some, however, had a preference for only one type of reward, leading to a dependency, a tendency to be dependent emotionally on parents, or to be coldly aloof or to be bound by rules. Kozeki warned against putting too much stress on one kind of reward, and suggested that teachers put more stress on moral and cooperative behaviour.

Entwistle looked at the development of another strain of research which looked at reward and praise. Too heavy a reliance on external rewards such as exams or vocations led to *extrinsic* motivation. More desirable is *intrinsic* motivation, where young people's natural interest and effort is reward enough. Over time, tests were developed to try to measure achievement motivation. These were rarely reliable, and self-reporting inventories were often more highly correlated with school and university achievement, being better predictors of success than prior attainment alone.

Entwistle himself in 1977 had identified four contrasting groups of students:

1 intrinsically motivated
2 competitive and self-confident
3 anxious and lacking in self-confidence
4 non-academically motivated.

He argued that the fourth group had *effort avoidance*, often citing 'boredom' as the reason for their disaffection. Rollett (1987) identified 'students of differing personality and motivational types [who] tackle[d] their academic work in different ways'. This led to a new focus in research into educational motivation, suggesting that it was more complex than originally thought and that different forms of motivation might lead to different forms of learning.

Entwistle cited Marton and Salijo (1984) who talked about 'deep' and 'surface' learning. Feelings of anxiety often push pupils towards the 'surface' approach while *intrinsic* motivation is closely aligned with the 'deep' approach. A third approach, the 'strategic', has been identified, often associated with learners who calculate what is necessary to pass exams, i.e. 'playing the examination game'.

The issues of success and failure are important in the context of motivation. Entwistle identified two groups of pupils in terms of how they attribute the cause of their success or failure. Pupils who use *external* attributions (e.g. bad luck, unfairness of the exam, boring nature of the task, etc.) are denying their own responsibility for the outcome. Those who use *internal* attributions (e.g. effort or strategy adopted, ability, etc.) are more inclined to take responsibility for their own learning.

Entwistle, however, urged caution in trying simply to move all children from external to internal attributions. He cited Weiner (1984) who suggests that attributing failure to strategy is likely to lead to continued effort and a search for new strategies but an attribution to ability might lead to an expectation of continued failure, a conclusion also reached some years later by Carol Dweck (1999). Effort and strategy can be altered, but the learner may feel that ability cannot. Pupils labelled 'less able' might be exhorted to try harder, but if they still fail, the only remaining attribution is more painful, and avoidance is the most common option. Corno (1986) proposed 'self-regulated learning' as the route to self-motivation, giving learners an awareness of learning itself and how they learn to give them more control.

Brophy (1987) developed two sets of strategies for motivating learners:

Strategies for motivating

General strategies
1 Stress value and relevance of school work to everyday life
2 Show that you expect pupils to enjoy learning
3 Treat tests as ways of checking pupils' progress

Specific strategies
1 Explain why you find a topic or idea interesting
2 Introduce topics or tasks in ways which arouse interest
3 Create suspense or stimulate curiosity
4 Make abstract content more personal, concrete or familiar
5 Present paradoxes or incongruities for discussion
6 Encourage pupils to relate topics to their own interests
7 Explain course objectives and help pupils set their own goals and targets
8 Provide full and informative feedback on performance
9 Teach problem-solving by personal example
10 Encourage metacognitive awareness of learning processes (Provide and discuss memory aids, and lead group discussions on alternative learning strategies)

(Adapted from Brophy (1987), in Entwistle
(1987, p.144))

Brophy was writing in 1987 but there are clear links, conceptually and pedagogically, with other work which was being developed around the same time (Perkins, 1993) and work which emerged later (Black and Wiliam, 1998). Entwistle suggested that 'good teaching itself can be seen as one of the most effective motivators' (1987, p. 144) and it is clear from Brophy's lists that he believes that pedagogy is inextricably linked to motivation. Thus sharing goals, providing 'full and informative' feedback, providing challenge, personal target-setting, problem-solving, teachers leading by example and metacognition, all have resonances with what is considered good practice in classrooms today. Even the idea of 'memory aids', so effectively presented by Tony Buzan in his work on *Mind Mapping* (1993), but often denigrated by some as superficial, are acknowledged by Brophy as important, provided that their rationale is discussed with pupils. Entwistle referred to the work of John Nisbet and Janet Schucksmith (1986) who coined the phrase 'metacognitive strategies' to describe 'the orchestrations of the component skills of learning' (p. 146). These ideas informed the ill-fated '10–14 Report' of 1986, which sought to address the problems of primary–secondary transition through the development of a common pedagogy (Boyd, 2005). Entwistle (1987) suggested that:

> [A]ll these developments in teaching are intended to provide pupils with the tools they need to take charge of their own learning – to avoid the trap of painful attributions of failure by seeing how their own strategies can be developed.
>
> (p. 146)

He concluded with a restatement of a truth which will be familiar to most teachers, '[T]he only lasting motivation is, after all, self-motivation' (p. 146).

The motivated school: is motivation the new discipline?

Alan McLean's contribution to the issue of pupil motivation and behaviour has spanned some 20 years. His leadership of the project which produced a staff development pack for teachers entitled *Promoting Positive Behaviour* was an early indication of his perceptiveness and his ability to look constructively at an issue which is often plagued by negativity and prejudice. In recent years, he has turned his attention to the issue of motivation, surveying the literature, working in schools, engaging teachers and school managers in a CPD context, and writing challengingly about the subject. For him the twin issues of *motivation* and *(in)discipline* need to be considered at the same time.

Alan McLean's first book, *The Motivated School* (2003), addressed a number of key issues which are central to Scottish educational policy, including Better Behaviour, Better Learning; Inclusion and Raising Attainment. It was also a controversial book, challenging as it does 'woolly thinking' on issues such as self-esteem, rewards and motivation to learn. It made an important contribution to the debate about effective schools and how they meet the needs of all of their pupils. It addressed the most complex problems of our time, including the causes of disaffection, the strategies schools use to help these young people to achieve their potential, the effects schools actually have on pupils' self-esteem and the desirability of intrinsic rather than extrinsic rewards. McLean is characteristically robust in his thesis that self-efficacy, rather than woolly concepts of self-esteem, is what schools should be trying to foster in young people. He raised many important ideas such as 'engagement', the role of 'ability' in learning, and explanations of why there is a gender imbalance in terms of attainment nationally.

However, the book suffered from being overly complex and theoretical, and, happily, has led to a follow-up from the same author, *Promoting Motivational Resilience* (2008). With its associated website, this book is a distillation of the hundreds of hours of work with schools and of in-service training with teachers, of the most up-to-date research and, gratifyingly, is now written in a more user-friendly style.

For McLean, 'Motivational resilience is the capacity to cope with setbacks, adversity, pressure and also power.' The aim of the book is to enable teachers to 'build up a motivational framework' and create a 'learning climate' in their classrooms. To this end, he identifies four *energisers* that 'impact on pupil engagement':

- **Engagement,** which is the process through which the teacher tries to get to know, value and connect with the learner.
- **Structure** refers to the clarity of pathways to achieving the learning goals.
- **Stimulation** comes from a curriculum that highlights the relevance of activities.
- **Feedback,** which is information that allows the learner to know how he or she is progressing.

In addition, there are *learner needs,* which McLean calls the 3As:

- *Affiliation* – our sense of getting along with others.
- *Agency* – our sense of getting ahead.
- *Autonomy* – our sense of self-determination.

McLean's thesis is that each child has a unique personality which shapes his or her thoughts, feelings and behaviour. These add up to *self-emotions,* which he claims can be 'mapped onto' the learner needs:

> *Self-belief – Agency*
> The factors underlying Agency include, firstly, ideas about ability. Pupils can see intelligence as fixed while others think their ability can be increased through effort (Dweck, 2000). Secondly, their explanations of progress, which can be optimistic or pessimistic (Seligman, 1995).
> *Self-esteem – Affiliation*
> Self-esteem tells us when our acceptance is low to motivate corrective action (Leary *et al.,* 1995)
> *Self realisation – Autonomy*
> This is marked in the classroom by our attitudes towards achievement that influence how we approach learning

McLean is only too aware of the complexities of the classroom. The fact that each young person has a unique personality might lead us to believe that teachers must have a different approach to the motivation of each pupil. This would be impracticable, and so he argues that there are a limited number of *learning stances* which adequately describe the behaviour of most pupils. Helpfully, he suggests a range of aspects of the classroom climate which can act as *energisers* or *drainers* to those pupils who adopt particular stances:

Table 5.1 Stance-specific energisers and drainers (from McLean, 2008)

Learning stance	Stance-specific drainers The don'ts	Stance-specific energisers The do's
Hiding	Don't give long periods of individual work, particularly written work. Don't use a 'blank sheet' approach.	Do negotiate private challenges. Do provide activities where they can get them recognition from peers. Do give a head start to let them contribute to the class discussion.
Opposing	Don't take it personally. Don't box or paint them into a corner.	Do try to find something you like about them. Do give high profile public responsibilities.
Quietly engaging	Don't use sarcasm.	Do respect their need for privacy and distance.
Energetically engaging	Don't allow them to be too competitive and bossy.	Do make them responsible for generating interest if they find the work boring.
Harmoniously engaging	Don't undermine their pro social behavior by unnecessary rewards.	Do make the responsibilities real by deciding them on the pupils' terms.
Exasperating	Don't distract them by overemphasising rewards. Don't suppress any calming activities.	Do track progress by positives, e.g. how many times they answered questions. Do give clear signals that prepare them to attend, particularly at transitions.
Alarming and draining	Don't let them spend too much time in 'passive entertainment'. Don't encourage them to vent their anger.	Do maintain familiar activities and routines. Do help them replace self-defeating language with more positive self-talk. Do use planning time to emphasise self-control.

The challenge implicit in McLean's analysis is that low motivation and poor pupil behaviour are the results of a mix of pupil and teacher actions and attitudes. The teacher, by being able to analyse the situation more productively, is in a better position to do the things which help create a positive classroom climate.

Perhaps the most significant contribution of McLean's book is the detailed analysis of these *stances* and the advice he gives teachers on how to deal with them in ways which are positive and affirming. His analysis is helpful in removing the confrontational paradigm, the teacher *versus* pupil scenario, which develops into a win–lose situation. Instead, by looking at behaviour through the lens of motivation, teachers are given insight and, therefore, strategies which they can use to promote a positive classroom climate.

Confidence and wellbeing: the keys to a motivated classroom?

Carol Craig's thesis (2003) is that 'confidence is ... central to what we achieve in life' (p. 2) and she attempts to reach a definition of it by considering related concepts such as self-esteem, self-efficacy and optimism. Her 'confidence formula' emerges as:

$$confidence = self\text{-}efficacy + optimism$$

In arriving at such a conclusion, Craig, controversially, offers a scathing critique of the way *self-esteem* has dominated the debate for so long, particularly in the United States, with, she believes, disastrous consequences for a whole generation. She, like Alan McLean, refers to the work of Martin Seligman and colleagues (1996), *The Optimistic Child*, which describes how in California in the 1960s, low self-esteem was identified by a prominent politician as the cause of social ills such as teenage pregnancy, crime, drug abuse and school underachievement. The problem encountered by the Task Force that was set up to study the issue of self-esteem was 'how low the associations between self-esteem and its [presumed] consequences are in research to date' (p. 11).

Craig describes how, notwithstanding a growing body of research which questions the link between self-esteem and particular outcomes, the UK Government has continued to promote it in a series of educational initiatives (p. 13). Craig cites the book by Jean Twenge, *Generation Me* (2006), which argues that after 20 years of praise and other attempts to boost self-esteem, American young people are more miserable than ever before. But if teachers in this country have also been told, like their American counterparts, that self-esteem is something they should try to boost in their pupils, what is to prevent a similar situation happening here? In other words, if low self-esteem has been seen to be associated with underachievement, but the evidence for the link is tenuous, what are teachers to do to create *confident individuals?*

The phrase preferred by Craig is *self-efficacy* (p. 72), coined by Albert Bandura, an American psychologist, in 1997. The key differences between this and self-esteem are that the former is goal-specific (not global) and is 'about agency or the ability to take action and achieve specific goals' (Craig, 2007). Bandura also argues that self-efficacy is facilitated by feelings of *optimism.* He links optimism to what we might call 'stickability' or perseverance, and cites the experience of James Joyce whose *Dubliners* was rejected by 22 publishers. He also suggests that self-efficacy can be developed by:

Mastery experiences	overcoming obstacles through perseverance
Vicarious experiences	role models can help others learn the skills
Social persuasion	being persuaded by others that 'they have what it takes'
Somatic and emotional states	learning to cope better with stress and improve your emotional state. (Craig, 2007, pp.73–74)

Perhaps the most helpful section of Carol Craig's book for teachers is the one in which she looks at what they can do to encourage feelings of self-efficacy. Many of the following will be familiar to teachers but one or two signify a change in emphasis from previous advice:

1 Be challenging.
2 Help students with goal setting.
3 Encourage students to see failure constructively.
4 Give feedback that encourages good strategies for improvement.
5 Give genuine encouragement.
6 Encourage students' self-reflection.
7 Get students to think and say ... I can.

Scottish teachers will already have made the links with Assessment is for Learning (2, 4 and 6); Determined to Succeed (1 and 7); and numbers 3 and 5 are fundamental to all classrooms. Indeed, these two, taken together, might involve the biggest change in perspective of all.

Craig draws on the work of Carol Dweck on *growth and fixed mindsets*. She cites Alan McLean's work in which he observes that too often pupils link failure with 'global factors' which suggest that it is 'inevitable'. Dweck's description of a fixed mindset, based on an outmoded concept of intelligence (see Chapter 10), is associated with such a view of failure. What teachers should do, argues Craig, is to help pupils to see failure as 'something they can put right with effort and the application of better strategies'. Thus, if we as teachers know that, in order to learn anything worthwhile, we have to be prepared to make mistakes and to fail, and if we know that intelligence is not fixed and predictable over time, we should share these insights with our pupils.

The corollary of this is that *praise* should not be given cheaply nor should it be given just for being 'right' or 'bright'. Praise should be given for application, for determination, for applying new strategies, and its aim should be to 'encourage a student to make the effort which leads to improvement' (p. 76).

Craig has developed a model of confidence. There are four elements:

Element	Watchwords
Self-efficacy	I can
Optimism	I will
Support from others	You will
Learning from others	We can

Her conclusions highlight 'the opportunities and pitfalls of aiming to foster young people's confidence in schools' (p. 176). She counsels against seeing confidence solely as a social skill; rather it is about self-belief and self-efficacy. This should warn us against attempts to introduce 'classes in confidence for students' (p. 177). Her advice is to 'create the conditions for young people's confidence to rise' (p. 177). This is best done by teachers modelling confidence, referring to real situations and looking and responding to demonstrated needs. Craig is very wary of any attempts which might be made to evaluate or assess confidence. She points to the tendency of formal education systems to examine, to test and to measure and feels that this could be counter-productive.

Craig's final point is one which is altogether more problematic. Her view that narcissism, brought on by an excessive concentration on raising the self-esteem of young people in the United States, has led to the emergence of the phenomenon of the 'fragile self' (Furedi, 2003) and a rise in mental health problems. Elsewhere, Craig warns of the use of praise and is concerned about schools where too much emphasis is placed on *programmes* designed to promote confidence in young people. For many Scottish teachers, it is not praise but the absence of it which concerns them. Too many pupils in their classes appear never to have been praised for anything. The Scottish psyche is ill at ease with praise: 'Ah kent yer faither' is a remark designed to take anyone down a peg or two if they are getting above themselves. What is more helpful from the Centre for Confidence and Wellbeing is less the denigration of praise and the dismissal of self-esteem than the exploration of how these concepts interact with others; with *self-theories* (Dweck), with *motivation* (McLean) and with *self-efficacy* (Bandura). Thus, instead of leaving teachers with the impression that they have been doing it all wrong when they used four-times-praise-to-one-time-criticism or when they tried to boost self-esteem by giving pupils a sense of achievement, the *Creating Confidence* handbook could be used to allow teachers to explore how their efforts might be most effectively targeted.

Principles of the motivated classroom

Motivation remains a complex issue especially when it is related, in a school setting, to (in)discipline and disruptive behaviour. There is a consensus that 'good teaching' is much more likely to improve motivation than any set of bullet points which can be generated on the issue. But, as this book demonstrates, 'good teaching' is a multi-faceted concept; we can recognise it when we see it but it is notoriously difficult to prescribe. What is clear is that *the motivated classroom* will be built on the following principles, but these alone may not be enough if other contextual factors (like 'setting', Chapter 8, or concepts of intelligence, Chapter 10) are not addressed:

- *Self-motivation* The key to motivation lies in the pupil's self-awareness. From Entwistle to Dweck, the emphasis is on self-motivation or *intrinsic* motivation. This can be achieved by involving pupils in the discussion or negotiation of learning outcomes, teaching them about the learning process itself and how intelligence works, and giving them access to a range of learning strategies which they can use when they encounter failure.
- *Praise* The use of praise is important in the learning process, but recently it has come in for some scrutiny. Teachers know that inappropriate praise can have the opposite effect to the intended. Public praise may cause embarrassment, resentment or even anger. Praise for work which is not perceived by the student as worthy will appear empty and insincere. And, as psychologists have suggested more recently, if the praise is only for being intelligent rather than for working hard to achieve certain goals, it can actually reinforce attitudes to learning which encourage pupils (especially 'more able' pupils) to give up rather than try harder. The message seems to be: use praise but use it judiciously, sincerely and for the right things.
- *Challenge and support* There is a concern among many teachers that many pupils are not being challenged. *A Curriculum for Excellence* implicitly recognised this when it added the principle of *depth* to those of breadth, balance, continuity, coherence and progression which had characterised the 5–14 curriculum. If a curriculum is too

exam-driven, if it promotes surface and rote learning; if it elevates knowledge acquisition above understanding, then many pupils will feel frustrated. If, in addition, the organisation of classes is based on these same examinations and tests derived from them, pupils may well be labelled (as As, Bs, Cs, etc.) and 'appropriate' work given to them. In the 1980s, work done by Mary Simpson on *differentiation* suggested that too often when teachers feel they have matched tasks to pupils' abilities, the pupils' perceptions are that the work is too easy. A motivated classroom is one where the level of challenge engages pupils, causes them to work hard and gives them a sense of achievement when they meet their goals.

POINTS FOR REFLECTION

1. Entwistle reviews some theories of motivation. What do you think of his argument?

2. McLean's work is attracting a lot of interest among schools. Why do you think his analysis is proving to be useful to teachers?

3. Do you think the principles of *the motivated classroom* are helpful to teachers?

6 The democratic classroom

> One thing seems clear: if all students are helped to the full unitization of their intellectual powers, we will have a better chance of surviving as a democracy...
> Jerome Bruner, *The Process of Education*

Citizenship has become a key issue in the twenty-first century. In Scotland there are concerns about lack of engagement with the political process while internationally the post 9/11 concerns about tolerance and co-existence have prompted a desire for citizenship education. In this chapter we look at developments in Scotland around the democratic classroom, as well as projects designed to promote specific aspects of citizenship.

Introduction: Citizenship in Scottish education

In 1944, a report by the Advisory Council on Education, *Training for Citizenship*, was published by the Scottish Education Department. In the section headed 'The Nature of the Problem', the report lists four priorities:

> Our conception of the purpose of training for Citizenship is the training of young people –
> (1) to become good husbands and wives and fathers and mothers;
> (2) to develop the spirit of responsibility and of tolerant co-operation with their fellows in work or leisure activities;
> (3) to take an intelligent and independent part in the affairs of the community, both local and national;
> (4) to have a sense of membership of the world community.
>
> (p. 4)

It has to be understood that this report was published during a World War and at a time when 'slum clearance' was becoming a part of social policy, but there was a determination that neither of these two factors should delay a policy on citizenship:

> These conditions (slums and poor housing) must rather be regarded as a challenge, and the vision of better conditions in the post-war world as an incentive, calling for increased effort.
>
> (pp. 4–5)

Citizenship had appeared as a 'basic function of our schools' in the Education Act 1872. The Advisory Council report recommended a five-year period of 'experiment and of deliberate striving towards a theory and practice in training for Citizenship' (p. 5).

The report went on to identify some key issues including:

The school as a community

Some of what we may feel are modern ideas are dealt with here, albeit in the language of the day. The 'tone' and 'distinctive atmosphere' of the school is regarded as important; the 'problem of backward children ... [may require] more creative work ... [to] relieve many such children of a sense of failure and frustration' (p. 7) and 'there is an urgent need to reduce the size of the class in the Primary school to a maximum of thirty' (p. 7). Some of the problems facing the system today were around then too, though in some cases the situation appears to have got worse in the intervening years. Primary–secondary discontinuity (Boyd, 2005) was an issue then too; 'the change from a single teacher in the Primary School to as many as six or seven specialists produces in some children mental perplexity and maladjustment ...'; some 60 years later, the problem remains but the number of teachers that an S1 pupils meets is likely to be double that in 1944. The report advocated leadership for pupils in the form of 'monitors' within a house system and based on the structures of the Scout and Guide movements. And the report advocated a programme of accelerated school building in which 'the classrooms should be made as airy and attractive as possible' (p. 8).

Aesthetic training

The bold claim was made that 'No education can be regarded as complete unless an attempt is made to develop in the child some aesthetic appreciation of Art, Music and the beauties of Nature. Imagination ought to be stimulated' (p. 11).

The rules of health

The report states that 'Health and happiness are intimately related' and 'physical training should form part of the daily routine in all schools'. This is particularly apposite in the early part of the twenty-first century, with concern over rising levels of obesity and a drive to require schools to have two hours of physical activity each week for every child.

The contribution of the individual school subject

The report looked at subjects, one by one, and made recommendations, which were clearly of their time, and timeless. The current debate about 'Britishness' and language fluency has echoes in the 1944 debate about Scots dialect; the report suggests that '[E]very good citizen should take a pride in the correct use of his native tongue' (p. 12) and condemns 'slovenly speech'. (The present writer can remember his parents, neither of whom had had a secondary school education in the 1920s and 1930s, being so concerned about his 'slovenly speech' and that of his sister, that they sent both of them to elocution classes in Drumchapel in the late 1950s.) Geography, History and Civics are all given special mention, but, essentially, the message was that all teachers are teachers of citizenship – to use the modern jargon, a genuine 'cross-cutting theme'.

Finally, almost as a footnote, the report recommends 'an extension of holiday facilities' and 'the provision of adequate playing fields'; thus the current emphasis on outdoor education and daily physical activity are not new either!

Educational theory: a justification for the democratic classroom

It has been argued that many of the early theories of learning, from Plato through the behaviourists to Piaget, suffered from the same defect, namely that 'the learner is depicted as a lone investigator' (Philips and Soltis, 2004, p. 53). This is attributed to the Western/liberal tradition, which has seen human development as moving from being individuals to members of society. Indeed, it is commonly believed by those who share this world view that individuals *chose* to form societies (cf. Rousseau's *Social Contract*). This has been challenged as a myth by those who believe that humans are innately social creatures and that our ancestors became rational *in* groups; they did not become rational and then form groups (Philips and Soltis, 2004, p. 54).

In the context of citizenship and the democratic classroom, the American philosopher and educationist John Dewey has made an important contribution to theory and practice:

> As a matter of fact every individual has grown up, and always must grow up, in a social medium. His responses grow intelligent, or gain meaning, simply because he lives and acts in a medium of accepted meanings and values. Through social intercourse, through sharing in the activities embodying beliefs, he gradually acquires a mind of his own.
>
> (Quoted in Philips and Soltis, 2004, p. 56)

For Dewey, school was a community but too much emphasis on individual learning meant that *understanding* was not achieved. Rote learning might give the illusion of understanding but the best way of learning was through communication with others.

It is not surprising then that Dewey was a prolific writer on the links between democracy and education. He advocated that schools should organise their practice on the principle of liberty by engaging pupils in self-directed learning. His view was that teachers should create an environment in which pupils were encouraged to think independently as well as considering the ideas of others. Indeed, he went so far as to propose that pupils could become citizens and make effective decisions for the good of democracy.

What we have to realise is that Dewey's ideas were seen as revolutionary at the time. The dominant pedagogy in the United States in the 1930s included recitation, rote learning and learned responses to teachers' questions. Pupils would chant, engage in choral repetition and recite passages of poetry by heart. Dewey and his followers were labelled 'progressives'. Along with Maria Montessori and her vision of the teacher as a facilitator of enquiry and exploration, Dewey's ideas ensured that progressive education remained popular in the United States in the 1940s. While Dewey's ideas had something of a resurgence in popularity in the 1970s, by the 1980s the national (and international) focus on *attainment* as measured by test scores and examination performance meant that progressive education became less popular among the public in general and among educational policy-makers.

Perhaps the most important advocate of social learning in the twentieth century was Lev Vygotsky who, working quite independently of Dewey's ideas, argued that much of what we learn we learn from others. For both Vygotsky and Dewey, language acquisition and development took place in social settings and were essentially about communication. Vygotsky saw the importance of *imitation* in learning, and in the United States Albert Bandura (1986) saw imitation as being at the heart of his 'social learning theory'.

Thus, the democratic classroom, seen in Scotland as an aspect of education for citizenship, has a strong theoretical underpinning. If democracies are as much about disagreement as they are about consensus, then young people need opportunities and skills to participate in debate and in decision-making. As they do so, they develop as learners and as citizens.

Democracy and the modern world: a new orthodoxy?

In her book *The Riddle of all Constitutions*, Susan Marks (2000) examines the claim that democracy has acquired the status of an 'international human right' (p. 1). She observes that there is an emerging view that '"democratic countries should do everything possible to promote democracy in the world" including military action' and warns that the 'risk of imperialism looms large'. Her 'democratic norm thesis' springs from an analysis of the new world order after the First World War when she suggests that 'international legal scholars ... began to propose that ... international law should be seen to require democratic government' (p. 37). The Versailles Treaty, post-colonial arrangements and the international recognition of human rights after the Second World War all emphasised the right to self-determination 'in a democratic fashion' (p. 38). This trend continued in the aftermath of the Cold War, so much so, argues Marks, that no longer are all forms of Government regarded as equal; 'democratic government is the only legal option' (p. 40). Her concern is that what is described here is at best a limited form of democracy – 'low intensity democracy' (p. 50). She does not argue that democracy should not be pre-eminent in the current world order; rather she is concerned that it might be imposed as the solution to all constitutional problems (p. 151).

The significance of Marks' thesis for teachers is that any approach in the classroom based on 'democracy good; all else bad' would be to over-simplify the situation around the world. What passes for democracy in many countries would not satisfy the most stringent tests which we might apply. Equally, there are times in our own country when the Government of the day does not appear to be listening to the views of its electorate. And if a country with no history of democracy moves towards some middle ground as an interim step, how are we to react? The problematic nature of internal governance is part of the context within which young people have to view events in the world.

Democracy in the modern world: values and processes

A Curriculum for Excellence has the development of young people as *responsible citizens* as one of its four purposes of education. This is in keeping with advice given to schools in Scotland in *Education for Citizenship in Scotland: A Paper for Discussion and Development* (www.scotland.org.uk/citizenship/index.asp) (Learning and Teaching Scotland, 2002). This paper emanated from the Advisory Council of Learning and Teaching Scotland (LTS) and contained a preface written by the chair of LTS which outlined the 'central idea' as:

... that young people should be enabled to develop capability for thoughtful and responsible participation in political, social and cultural life.

(p. 3)

The paper argues that 'young people learn most about citizenship by being active citizens' (p. 3) and suggests, in terms not dissimilar to those of the enterprise literature, that 'the development of an open, participatory ethos' within educational establishments is the ultimate objective.

The report poses four main questions:

- What do we mean by 'citizenship'?
- Why is 'education for citizenship' important?
- What should education for citizenship do for young people?
- What does effective education for citizenship involve in practice – for the curriculum, for school and early education centres and for communities?

(p. 5)

The reader does not have to look beyond the Introduction to find the first reference to 'democratic processes'. Admittedly, the notion of democracy had been implied in references to 'participation' and 'active citizenship', but here the explicit reference echoes the words of the National Priorities which referred to 'citizenship in a democratic society'. There is no doubt that democracy is, for citizens of Scotland, the norm, but it is also true that, for citizens of other countries, this is not the case. We may cherish our democratic values, but must also recognise that not everyone shares them. If, when conflicts arise across the world, some of our enemies do not share our commitment to democracy, is it legitimate to assume that democracy is better than other forms of government? Can we be certain that any democratic government will always act fairly and justly in the interests of all of its people? Are we confident that democracy always ensures that individual voices are listened to and that human rights are respected?

The report acknowledges that 'Scotland and the rest of the UK exist in a rapidly changing world' (p. 6) and that among the challenges facing us are 'the distribution of power' and the 'inequalities between the economically rich and poor' (p.6). If these issues are to be addressed, argues the report, it will be done in part by the creation of an education system intent on:

> fostering a modern democratic society, whose members have a clear sense of identity and belonging, feel empowered to participate effectively in their communities and recognise their roles and responsibilities as global citizens.

(p. 7)

The rationale for the report is boldly stated but not without its ambiguities. It argues that 'everyone should be recognised as a citizen, in a variety of senses, from birth' (p. 8) with rights that are 'well described in the UN Convention on the Rights of the Child'. This is interesting in the light of recent debate on the status of immigrants, particularly those seeking asylum. Partly as a response to the growing threat of terrorism, the concept of British citizenship is being refined, with caveats about fluency in English and knowledge of British institutions being added. The report talks of 'reciprocal' rights and responsibilities and acknowledges potential conflicts among various groups within a democratic society. Indeed, it argues that the very processes and strategies available to resolve disputes are at the heart of a democratic society. It is in this context that the school is seen to be an important part of 'education for citizenship' (p. 9).

Those readers who have knowledge of how schools work may already have spotted the paradox at work here. How can schools which are themselves hierarchical organisations promote active democracy? Put more simply, if schools are not themselves democratic in their processes, can they foster 'active and responsible citizens' (p. 9)? Is the concept of a *democratic classroom* simply Utopian when many teachers are concerned about the downward pressure of examination results, when class sizes in many stages and subject areas are still around 30 and when, in many schools, poor motivation and low-level misbehaviour are perceived to be obstacles to learning?

The 'Examples of learning outcomes related to skills and competences for citizenship' may not be seen as a help to these teachers:

> As a result of their learning experiences, young people should become progressively more able to:

- work independently and in collaboration with others to complete tasks requiring individual or group effort as appropriate
- locate, handle, use and communicate information and ideas, using ICT as appropriate
- question and respond constructively to the ideas and actions of others in debate and/or in writing
- contribute to discussion and debate in ways that are assertive and, at the same time, attentive and respectful of others' contributions
- make informed decisions in relation to political, community and environmental issues
- persevere, where appropriate, in the face of setbacks and practical difficulties
- negotiate, compromise, or assist others to understand and respect difference, when conflict occurs, recognising the difference between consensus and compliance.

(p. 13)

While it is not entirely clear whether each of these bullet points is actually a learning outcome or part of the learning process, what is true is that the list contains very few elements which cannot be found in other initiatives, notably enterprise. However, the picture of the democratic classroom which emerges is one where pupils work variously in pairs or groups or individually using information and communicating with others orally or in writing. They are making informed choices, having engaged in respectful but robust debate with others, not giving up at the first sign of difficulty, and negotiating with others on the basis of mutual respect.

Democracy and citizenship?

Ross Deuchar has argued that the term 'citizenship', commonly used in the English education system in the late nineteenth and early twentieth centuries, disappeared sometime after the Second World War. While other countries, notably the United States, have had 'civics' on the school timetable for some time, there was no enthusiasm, it seems, in Britain for a subject called citizenship.

Under Mrs Thatcher in the late 1980s, a discussion arose initiated by Douglas Hurd, who advocated active citizenship as part of a 'moral re-alignment' (Deuchar, 2007, p. 25) This was altogether a more serious contribution than that of his Cabinet colleague Norman Tebbitt, who famously tried to reduce British citizenship for those of Asian origin to a matter of which international cricket team they would support! Proposals were made for citizenship to become a part of the school curriculum, but there was little enthusiasm from the teaching profession. Within the National Curriculum in England and Wales, citizenship emerged as one of a number of cross-curricular themes which did not become embedded in the practice of most schools, partly as a result of the emphasis on examination performance within the traditional subjects.

In the late 1990s, a number of forces combined to put citizenship back on the educational agenda. Deuchar lists the Labour victory in 1997, the 1998 Human Rights Act, Devolution in Scotland and Wales, constitutional reform within the Labour Party itself and the emergence of the so-called 'third way' from the Blair Government, as some of these forces (Deuchar, 2007, p. 25). The early part of the twenty-first century saw a number of cataclysmic events which sharpened this focus. The attack on the twin towers of the World Trade Centre in New York in 2001 had a profound effect not just on the American world view but on subsequent events which have led to a polarisation in attitudes world-wide. The Iraq War and its effect on public opinion; the Make Poverty History campaign and successive G8 summit; the accession of former communist Eastern Bloc countries to the European Union; a growth in asylum seekers in the UK (and across the world); and, above all else, the growth in terrorism world-wide, in particular the use of suicide bombing within cities and other population centres, all combined to generate a new debate on what it is to be a citizen in the modern world. The debate became complicated by the inter-relationship of religious belief and citizenship. In particular, Islam began to attract opprobrium and it became, in the minds of some in the media, an ever-present epithet of fundamentalism.

The bombings in London in 2005 were, perhaps, the catalyst in the UK. The shocking truth that the bombers had been born, and educated, in the UK sparked off a period of introspection. How could British citizens kill fellow Britons (and others)? How had they become radicalised? Why did their religious fundamentalism appear to override their citizenship? What was the role of the Iraq War in turning neighbour against neighbour? And if some of these young people had been 'brainwashed' by clerics and others, what role could education play in re-defining and clarifying citizenship?

Deuchar's chapter on 'Creating a democratic culture' (Deuchar, 2007, pp. 69–95) takes pupil councils as a case study. He reminds us of the legislative framework, beginning with the United Nations Convention on the Rights of the Child, particularly article 29:

> The right to an education which prepares her/him for an active responsible life as an adult in a free society.

Deuchar cites the Learning and Teaching Scotland report of 2002, which proposes that 'pupil participation should be developed' and offers pupil councils as an example of how this might be achieved (p. 15). He cites the experience of Denmark, which in 1996 enacted a statutory requirement for secondary schools to create pupil councils. He lists another seven countries in Europe which have made similar moves, although stopping short of legislation. But he also refers to research which criticises pupil councils for being restricted in their discussions to the 'charmed circle of lockers, dinners and uniform' (Baginsky and Hannam, 1999). The warning is clear: tokenism is no substitute for real participation in decision-making. Deuchar's own research sample included schools with 'well-established school councils' (Deuchar, 2007, p. 73). In primary schools, council meetings were attended and the following conclusions emerged:

- Pupil councils often talk about 'wider issues relating to social values'.
- Pupil councils get involved in community projects.
- Democratic elections are used to create pupil councils.
- Teachers tend to take a purely facilitating role.
- The commitment of teachers varies.
- The pupil council is often a steering committee for other pupil forums.
- Pupils not on the council seem motivated and encouraged by its work.

(pp. 75–76)

The contribution of councils in secondary schools was less encouraging. Firstly, the impact of the council seems to vary with the age of the pupils; senior pupils get the chance to participate in social projects while young pupils are more likely to concentrate on more mundane issues. Overall, non-council members were less positive about the council in the secondary sector.

The Holocaust: a suitable case for treatment?

Despite the atrocities which have followed, including genocide in Africa, Asia and in Europe itself, the Holocaust remains pre-eminently the most potent symbol of 'man's inhumanity to man'. As such, the Holocaust appears on the curriculum in many countries across the world and is a central part of many citizenship courses. In 2005, a team of Scottish researchers was commissioned by the Scottish Executive Education Department (SEED) to conduct research on whether Holocaust education has an impact on pupils' citizenship values and attitudes and, if so, whether it ought to be an important element of citizenship education. In particular, the researchers wished to find out whether Holocaust education in primary and in secondary school had a impact on young people's attitudes and values across the transition from primary to secondary school, and whether such values applied to minorities in contemporary Scotland.

There were three schools in the research project: two primary and one secondary. In the case of the primaries, the pupils were interviewed before lessons on the Holocaust and immediately afterwards, and then some 10 months later when they had moved to secondary school. In the secondary school, pupils who had not received the lessons on the Holocaust were interviewed as a kind of 'control group'. Staff were also interviewed about pedagogy and resources used in their lessons.

The findings of the research were interesting. In the words of the report, 'there was some notable *improvement* [my emphasis] in pupils' attitudes and values immediately after the lessons on the Holocuast in Primary 7, though it was not universal'. This improvement was maintained (though not as strong) some 10 months later when the pupils were in S1 and there was evidence that pupils who had studied the Holocaust had 'more positive values and attitudes' than those who had not studied it. Finally, the researchers were confident that there was evidence that it was, in fact, the study of the Holocaust which was responsible for the improvement in pupils' attitudes.

The report contains the most up-to-date account of Holocaust education in Scotland. Its aim, contrary, perhaps, to the popular view, is not to *eradicate* anti-semitism. There is a more pragmatic aim based on the belief that Holocaust education will never change everyone's views. Thus, it sets out to *inoculate* the population against anti-semitic propaganda and ensure that anti-semitism is the preserve only of a 'disaffected and politically insignificant rump' (Short and Reed, 2004). The content of Holocaust education in Scotland has, traditionally, included the story of Anne Frank and the testimonies of Holocaust survivors. More recently, say the researchers, this has been supplemented by resources focusing on more recent genocides and on contemporary racism and discrimination.

One finding of the report has an important implication for schools in Scotland in the twenty-first century. The authors found 'a worrying hostility towards English people' among the pupils surveyed. This was reinforced in 2007 by the findings of a YouthLink Scotland survey of 11–16 and 17–25 year olds in Scotland, reported in *The Sunday Herald* (Money, 'Pride and Prejudice', Sunday 16.12.07). The focus of the research was how Scots feel about being young in Scotland. It suggested that only 28% of 17–15 year olds felt that more should be done to help other nationalities settle in Scotland (a drop of 9% since 2005) and a third of 11–16 year olds felt that there were too many immigrants in Scotland (an increase of 8% since 2005). However among the 17–25 year olds, there was an increase of 35% in those who felt there were too many immigrants.

It is interesting that the anti-immigrant sentiments are higher among the 17–25 year olds than the 11–16 year olds. This may well support the Maitles thesis (Maitles *et al.*, 2005) that education in schools can have a positive effect on young people's attitudes. However, it may be that, while the positive gains can bridge the gap between primary and secondary school, these gains may not survive the transition to work (or, indeed, to unemployment). In an interview accompanying the main report of the survey's findings, the *Sunday Herald* sought the views of young people. One suggested that immigrant workers were taking jobs, albeit low-paid ones, from young people in rural areas, while another young person suggested that media portrayal of immigrants was to blame. They were often portrayed as 'spongers', yet Jamie O'Neill (21) felt that migration was 'a two-way street' since a lot of young Scots went overseas to find work.

The implications of the research of Maitles and colleagues, and the YouthLink Scotland survey, are stark and the *democratic classroom* may be able to help. The same YouthLink Scotland survey suggested that a worrying percentage of young people have a low opinion of the impact of the Scottish Parliament on life in Scotland. The high percentage of those who said 'don't know' as to whether the Scottish Parliament had made an impact on life in Scotland, or who neither agreed nor disagreed (55% of 11–16s and 66% of 17–25s) suggests that political awareness or enthusiasm is not high. The challenge of *A Curriculum for Excellence* in producing young people who are *responsible citizens* cannot be underestimated.

The principles of the democratic classroom

There is an undeniable irony in trying to postulate the democratic classroom within the confines of a school – perhaps one of the least democratic of our public institutions. The management structures of Scottish schools, even after the so-called McCrone enquiry (2001), are hardly less hierarchical than they were before. Some posts have disappeared (notably Assistant Headteacher and Assistant Principal Teacher) but others have been created (Principal Teacher in primary school, and, in some schools, Senior Depute).

However, many schools have taken considerable steps to change their culture to a more collegiate one, cutting across traditional posts and responsibilities and allowing staff to work in teams. Many of these same schools try to operate on the basis of *distributed leadership,* where any individual can take the lead on an issue in which s/he has particular expertise or experience. Thus, in these schools, the democratic classroom could flourish in the context of a culture which aims to promote creativity and leadership at all levels in the organisation.

- *Promoting critical thinking* Young people who can think for themselves, who can read and view critically the messages which come their way in the press, the broadcast media, the Internet, advertising and the rest, must surely be a desirable outcome of any education system in a democratic country. Opportunities to listen to opposing points of view, to engage with current and topical issues, to make connections in their learning across disciplines, seem to be part of *the democratic classroom*. Protocols about how to engage in debate and discussion are referred to in chapter 9, but it is clear that thinking is at the heart of being a citizen. Synthesising is a skill which will be in demand in the twenty-first century and being able to weigh up arguments, sort out fact from opinion and distinguish information from propaganda, are all going to be part of citizenship in the modern world. These are the complex skills which teachers can plan as part of their pupils' learning; they are also the kinds of skills any relevant assessment system should be concentrating on.

- *Pupil participation in decision-making* Pupil talk, cooperative learning and thinking are dealt with in various places in this book. But citizenship may well require more than this. If politics is about decision-making, then young people need to be given opportunities to make choices, to evaluate the outcomes and to look at the alternatives to their chosen course of action. If, for example, health education is about equipping young people to make 'informed choices', then it is not enough simply to provide the information. The process of making choices, the ways one can weigh up possibilities, the responsibilities involved (not just the rights) are of crucial importance. Some choices may seem personal and individual but may well have consequences which affect others. Many others will be taken as part of a group, a community or society. There are plenty of school contexts in which making choices can take place, and schools should do more than pay lip-service to pupil involvement in decision-making. In the classroom, opportunities abound should we wish to take them, from the topics being studied, the learning goals, the criteria for success, the learning approaches, the media being used, the kind of feedback to the class, the assessments, and so on. Class rules and conduct, relationships and interaction, actions and consequences are all part of the fabric of the democratic classroom. The greater the involvement of the pupils, the more ownership they will have of their learning and of their conduct in the classroom.

- *Confronting controversial issues* It is easy to avoid controversial issues. Classrooms can be embarrassing places in which to try to deal with some of the big issues facing young people in the modern world. Sometimes, we, as teachers, are not best placed to facilitate learning in certain contexts, and we have to bring others into the classroom who have more experience or more relevant expertise. There are sensibilities among the pupils, our colleagues, parents and others. Therefore, sensitive subjects should be introduced with this knowledge in mind, and prior consultation, information and explanation may well be required. But education cannot escape controversial issues: Shakespeare's treatment of anti-semitism in *The Merchant of Venice*; the Highland Clearances in Scottish history; the atomic bomb in physics; alcohol and tobacco consumption in Health Education; even team sports versus individual fitness and wellbeing in PE: all have controversial elements, which can either be 'air-brushed' out or can be the focus of learning. David Perkins has suggested that too much of our teaching is 'tame'. Perhaps this is one way, in controlled conditions, we can allow it to be a little 'wilder'.

POINTS FOR REFLECTION

1 Can democracy be taught effectively in a non-democratic environment? How could schools become more democratic places?

2 Do you think that citizenship is a concept with which teachers should be expected to grapple?

3 Are controversial issues such as the Holocaust suitable for classrooms?

4 What do you think of the principles of *the democratic classroom?*

7 The enterprising classroom

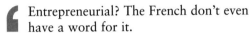

> Entrepreneurial? The French don't even
> have a word for it.
>
> **Attributed to George W. Bush;**
> **probably apocryphal**

Determined to succeed

Educational initiatives, historically, have liked enigmatic titles. *Determined to Succeed* works on a number of levels. All young people should have the opportunity, and the motivation, the drive, to do well. One could argue that all human beings are 'hard-wired' to learn successfully. The brain's *raison d'être*, after all, is learning and it has almost unlimited capacity to do so. But we know that, for a number of reasons, to do with poverty, disadvantage, lack of care, of nurture, of love and stimulation, many children grow up apparently pre-determined to fail. By the time some of them arrive at nursery, a lot of damage has been done. It is not, as Reuven Feuerstein (Feuerstein *et al.*, 2002) reminds us, irreversible, but for some the problems which have begun so early become compounded, and 'remedial' interventions do not reverse the damage. So the irony in the title serves as a reminder that the concepts which underpin enterprise education must be applied as soon as the learner enters the education system, at whatever age.

The Scottish Executive Education Department's website reminds us that 'Determined to Succeed is not another initiative; it is here to stay.' The seminal report *Determined to Succeed* was published in 2002. It was the work of an influential group, chaired by the then Deputy Minister for Education and Young People, Nicol Stephen, with headteachers, a director of education, representatives from the Scottish Executive Education Department, curriculum bodies and Scottish Enterprise, and key business people. Among the business people was the driving force behind the whole initiative, the Scottish businessman and philanthropist Sir Tom Hunter. The group's remit was:

> To assess the effectiveness of Education for Work and Enterprise in Schools, in preparing young people for the world of work and encouraging an enterprising culture in later life; and to examine the scope to improve Education for Work and Enterprise in fully supporting Scotland's priorities for education, and its economic success.

This remit put enterprise education firmly in the education-for-work arena. Indeed, the opening paragraph of the report stated:

> The ultimate goal of Enterprise in Education must be the creation of successful businesses, jobs and prosperity.
>
> (p. 6)

The impetus for this examination of enterprise in education was two-fold: the Scottish Executive's publication *Smart, Successful Scotland* (2001), which had identified a need for greater 'entrepreneurial dynamism' in Scotland: and the Scottish Executive's publication *Global Entrepreneurship Monitor, Scotland* (2002), which put Scotland in the lowest of three bands of entrepreneurial nations world-wide (although, interestingly, Japan, Singapore, and Germany, were also in this band). The statistics on business start-ups were cited in *Determined to Succeed*, showing that 'Scotland performs poorly against the rest of the UK (although similar to Wales and Northern Ireland)' (p. 9). While these figures seem less than conclusive, the conclusion was unequivocal:

> More young people need to have the opportunity to meet successful young entrepreneurs and see self-employment as a career option.
>
> (p. 9)

The report moved straight to Conclusions (since there was an accompanying *Evidence Report* which provided the detailed justification). The first recommendation was far-reaching:

> Every pupil from P1 to S6 must have an entitlement to enterprise education on an annual basis, and, in addition, pupils in S5 and S6 should have an entitlement to case studies based on local or Scottish businesses.
>
> (p. 12)

The report proceeds to take each of its 20 recommendations and flesh them out. In the case of the first recommendation, the report praised the work going on within the Schools Enterprise Programme but was critical of the fact that, despite this, 'too few young people have the opportunity to experience enterprise activities' (p. 16). While there continued to be an emphasis on 'business people as advisers and mentors', a new emphasis emerged. The creation of an 'enterprise ethos' and a 'pro-enterprise culture' was part of the Impact section for recommendation number 1. The explicit reference to the 'involvement of young people through people councils' emphasised the link between enterprise and citizenship.

In the report, which was peppered with colour photographs of Scottish entrepreneurs, Learning and Teaching Scotland (LTS) was given responsibility for reviewing guidance on work experience, SEED with commissioning research into part-time work undertaken by pupils at school, and Careers Scotland (along with LTS) with producing materials and resources to assist with the sharing of good practice. The Scottish Qualifications Authority (SQA) was directed, with LTS, to improve provision of Enterprise in Education within the framework of National Qualifications and there was a recommendation that 'Enterprise in Education must be included in Initial Teacher Education Programmes' (p. 46) as well as one which sought to have Enterprise Education available as part of the CPD of every teacher 'at least once every two years' (p. 48).

This report, with its case studies of good practice in schools, was one of the most hard-hitting and direct of any educational policy document in recent years. The use of the word 'must' in every one of its 20 recommendations was unprecedented. Not a single relevant public body or agency was left untouched by the recommendations; even HMIE were given the task of producing 'a set of Quality Indicators for Enterprise in Education' (p. 13). This was clearly a Review Group with some 'clout'; the question now was: how would schools create an enterprise ethos and what would a pro-enterprise culture look like?

The enterprising school

The Enterprising School (2005) was an attempt to answer these very questions. It was a publication from the Centre for Studies in Enterprise, Career Development and Work (Enterprising Careers) based in the Education Faculty of the University of Strathclyde. The Foreword argues that 'Through Enterprise Education we are attempting to change the culture in education and the mindset of educators ...' Ironically, the co-author of these words is none other than Douglas Osler, the former HM Chief Inspector of Schools and head of an organisation which many teachers would claim has, through its insistence on attainment targets, quality indicators and external inspection regime, made the classroom a much less enterprising place than it should be.

However, the report goes on to define enterprise as:

> ... a process where those involved are encouraged to adopt a can-do attitude and take responsibility for providing positive solutions to a real life challenge. The vision for success is agreed and the relevance and purpose of the task is understood.
>
> (Centre for Studies in Enterprise, Career Development and Work, 2005, p. 6)

So how should teachers rise to the enterprise challenge? The idea has some powerful champions, none more influential than Sir Tom Hunter, the billionaire entrepreneur and philanthropist who has, more than most, put his money where his mouth is to help schools engage with the enterprise philosophy. He was a member of the influential Review Group whose report gave the initiative its title (*Determined to Succeed: A Review of Enterprise in Education*, 2002) and which set out a number of recommendations as to how Scotland could get out of its low TEA (Total Entrepreneurial Activity) banding through a national educational strategy. The recommendations were not specifically aimed at the classrooms but did advocate that 'enterprise education be part of the Initial Teacher Education programmes and that serving teachers be given opportunities to participate in enterprise training 'at least once every two years' (p. 13).

The Enterprising School attempts to describe the characteristics of Enterprising People (p. 5):

Enterprising People are:

- confident ■ self aware/aware of others
- team players ■ decision makers
- responsible ■ driven to achieve ■ independent
- creative ■ able to use initiative
- positive ■ good communicators ■ flexible
- risk takers ■ resilient
- co-operative ■ able to cope with change

And goes on to outline the things an enterprising school would focus on (p. 13):

The Enterprising School
It prepares young people for life as earners and citizens, because it focuses on:

- relevance to real life ■ value and skills
- purpose – learning in a real context
- encouraging responsibility
- active and participative learning ■ reflecting society
- business links ■ community links
- involving parents and families ■ addressing change
- learning how to learn

However, the report does not reach the level of the classroom, except implicitly. It does address the issue of 'How we Learn' (p. 17):

> It is about teaching 'with' and not 'at', through teachers sharing responsibility for learning. It is about open discussions sharing ideas, using interactive approaches. Putting learning in a real context with a real purpose will give purpose to their learning. They will become independent learners as a result.

The issue of *independent* learning is key to the enterprising classroom – as it is to many of the classrooms described in this book. Vygotsky's dictum, quoted in Fisher (2001), sums up the link between independent learning and cooperative learning:

> What the child does in cooperation with others he will learn to do alone.
>
> (Fisher, 2001, p. 130)

The emphasis on peer- and self-assessment in the formative classroom has this end in mind also, namely the development of the child as an independent learner. In the thinking classroom, Art Costa's notion of thinking *interdependently* addresses the apparent paradox: how can cooperative learning foster independent learning? It is Vygotsky's theory of social constructivism which stated that a child learns to think through social experience, particularly, though not exclusively, through the interaction between the child and an adult (a mediator).

Thus, when *The Enterprising School* turns its attention to enterprising people, it is not surprising that similar characteristics emerge. Young people, it is suggested, should be encouraged to:

- take responsibility for their own learning and participate in the learning process
- make decisions, take ownership and become independent learners, co-operating to achieve
- use formative assessment techniques which will enable them to self-assess and move on in their own learning
- voice their opinion, be listened to and know that their opinions are valued

- understand that what they are learning is relevant to their lives
- understand the bigger picture and where they and their school fits
- understand that they can effect policies, decisions and opinions
- look for opportunities to work with business/community to gain valuable experience of the world of work.

(p. 21)

It is clear from this list that the authors of this report were trying to define best practice (Foreword) and they highlight many of the key principles which recur throughout this book:

- Independent learning
- Cooperative learning
- Formative assessment
- Democratic learning/values
- Understanding
- Global education
- Citizenship

The final bullet point in their list is a reminder of the origins of enterprise education, and of the paradox which underpins it. Deuchar (2007) has explored this dilemma and we will return to it later in this chapter.

The final sections of *The Enterprising School* deal with the practical issues of implementation and where the whole initiative might lead. A central element of implementation is 'learning *how* we do it' (p. 29). The concept of *metacognition* has already been introduced in this book, but the list of elements associated with independent learning in *The Enterprising School* is interesting:

- learn and to apply their learning to real life
- assess their own skills, know strengths and move forward
- achieve in real life situations and have ambition to succeed on their own terms
- work with others, co-operate, negotiate and compromise whilst building on one another's strengths and learning from one another
- use creative and critical thinking skills to make decisions and take responsibility for them
- use initiative and be independent

- communicate effectively – written, oral and ICT
- put their knowledge to practical use – e.g. functional literacy, numeracy and ICT
- adapt to change, be flexible and practice resilience
- take moderate risk and learn from failure
- be positive and develop a 'can-do' attitude
- problem solve.

(p. 29)

It is clear that, while in this document there is undoubtedly an over-use of bullet-pointed lists, this one is the most explicit attempt to define enterprise education without locating it in a business or world-of-work context.

The next section in the report offers four 'models for implementation' – Business, Citizenship, World of Work and Curriculum – reinforcing the message that enterprise education is more than simply about preparation for work. Instead, the report ends with the injunction that:

> Learning should be effective, engaging and enjoyable. It is not just about what we do, but also how we do it, that counts.
>
> (p. 41)

In many ways, *The Enterprising School* is an entirely up-beat, positive document but it is also light on specifics. It wishes enterprise not to be seen as another initiative, but tries to portray it as a 'culture change'. However, enterprise itself as a concept is more complex than this, and has been the subject of recent research in Scotland.

Enterprise: ideas for schools

In 2007, the Centre for Studies in Enterprise, Career Development and Work (Enterprising Careers) produced a 260-page A4 document entitled *Enterprising Ideas for Secondary Schools*. The foreword, by Linda Brownlow, the Centre's co-director, began with a summary of the then state of thinking about enterprise in education:

> Our young people need to have a clear purpose and a 'can-do' attitude to allow them to make the most of any opportunities in a personal, work or community context. They need to be flexible, creative, resourceful and prepared to take the initiative, and it is

widely acknowledged that enterprise education can help to foster these skills and attributes.

(Foreword)

This represents a subtle shift from a concept of enterprise education which focuses on the world of work and entrepreneurship to enterprise education which is about an enterprising approach to learning and teaching. Indeed, the Foreword goes on to say:

> Enterprise education is moving from a project-based initiative involving business, social or community *events* [my emphasis] to an overall approach to teaching and learning. Teachers recognise the need to work in an enterprising way – motivating students and ensuring that the curriculum is relevant and purposeful for all.
>
> (Foreword)

The first section of the document contains a helpful diagram which seeks to connect 'Enterprising Learning and Teaching' to 'A Curriculum for Excellence' (see page 110).

Thus, the concept of the enterprising school is seen as integral to the development of:

- successful learners
- confident individuals
- effective contributors
- responsible citizens.

However, the school is not an island, and the roles of the learners, the parents/guardians, teachers, businesses and communities are spelled out. The claim being made is that the four purposes of A Curriculum for Excellence can be 'delivered' through an enterprising approach, and in so doing the following will be achieved:

- relevance to the world around
- added value to the curriculum
- development of a positive ethos
- integration of the curriculum.

It might be said that this is quite a claim, but it is certainly indicative of the journey from enterprise education to an enterprising approach to learning and teaching.

Enterprising Learning and Teaching

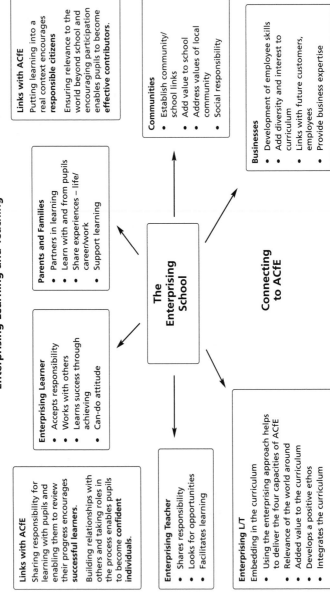

Links with ACfE

Putting learning into a real context encourages **responsible citizens**

Ensuring relevance to the world beyond school and encouraging participation enables pupils to become **effective contributors.**

Communities

- Establish community/ school links
- Add value to school
- Address values of local community
- Social responsibility

Businesses

- Development of employee skills
- Add diversity and interest to curriculum
- Links with future customers, employees
- Provide business expertise

Parents and Families

- Partners in learning
- Learn with and from pupils
- Share experiences – life/ career/work
- Support learning

Enterprising Learner

- Accepts responsibility
- Works with others
- Learns success through achieving
- Can-do attitude

The Enterprising School

Connecting to ACfE

Links with ACfE

Sharing responsibility for learning with pupils and enabling them to review their progress encourages **successful learners.**

Building relationships with others and taking roles in the process enables pupils to become **confident individuals.**

Enterprising Teacher

- Shares responsibility
- Looks for opportunities
- Facilitates learning

Enterprising L/T

Embedding in the curriculum

- Using the enterprising approach helps to deliver the four capacities of ACfE
- Relevance of the world around
- Added value to the curriculum
- Develops a positive ethos
- Integrates the curriculum

The enterprise agenda: a research perspective

Ross Deuchar's (2007) research included case studies of 'teachers' practice and [the] pupils perceptions' in the context of enterprise education. His central argument is the relationship between enterprise and citizenship, and he draws on a wide range of literature to support his thesis. He cites Oliver and Heater (1994), who described the school as a 'micro-social or political community', making the teachers' task of reconciling ethical and professional demands very difficult. Deuchar gives the example of the pressure felt by teachers by successive Governments' emphasis on examination success as the main criterion for judging the success of schools, leading to the compilation of exam 'league tables' (Deuchar, 2007, p. 7). If the teacher believes that s/he is educating the whole child, that 'achievement' is the focus, not narrow examination attainment; this poses a dilemma and potentially results in conflicting priorities. Deuchar refers to the research of Howard Gardner and colleagues into *Good Work* (2001). The first book emanating from Gardner *et al.*'s research project was sub-titled 'When Excellence and Ethics Meet' and looked at the issues through a series of interviews with Chief Executive Officers (CEOs) and other senior executives in the fields of journalism and genetics. One of their most striking findings, referred to by Deuchar, was the attitudes of young professionals at an early stage in their career. They knew that they should be guided by ethical principles but they were aware that by so doing they might compromise their promotion prospects, especially if rivals were not behaving ethically. Thus they were prepared to put ethical considerations on hold, so to speak, until their careers were secure. Deuchar suggests that teaching is not immune from such dilemmas: teachers may have 'strong professional and ethical goals' (p. 8) but the 'marketisation' of education, where pupils/parents may be seen as customers or consumers, means that teachers may become confused or frustrated about their roles (p. 9).

Thus when enterprise education is promoted in schools, some teachers may be suspicious of the underlying motives. Deuchar discusses what might be called the Davies' Dilemma, where teachers have to try to promote both civic values and competition, hence Deuchar's focus on the links between citizenship and enterprise.

His analysis of 'the nature of enterprise education in Britain' (p. 23) is interesting. He suggests that business enterprise projects or community-based projects are the most common manifestations of enterprise in schools. He cites research carried out by the Enterprise and Industry Education Unit at Durham University Business School in 1993 which indicated that 'children should emerge from enterprise projects more motivated, confident, creative, flexible, able to cope with failure, able to work in teams and willing to take risks' (Deuchar, 2007, p. 23). There is no mention here of business start-ups or entrepreneurship *per se,* but the kinds of generic skills and dispositions which permeate more recent Scottish publications. Deuchar argues that there persists in Britain a tendency for schools to be scapegoated for the country's relative lack of economic success and this in turn leads to a 'business enterprise model' (p. 23). He makes reference to the work of Ball (1984), who saw this as a cause for concern, and more recent writers, including Shacklock (2000), who have tried to widen the debate by identifying the enterprising teacher as one who 'focuses on enabling greater student autonomy, focuses teaching on relevant experiences, encourages teamwork and a focus on student review and self-assessment' (Deuchar, 2007: p23). Deuchar sees this kind of perspective and the content of the more recent Scottish publications as heralding a model of enterprise education 'as a means of both economic and social entrepreneurship'. A key issue for schools, therefore, is where the balance is to be struck between these two models and, therefore, what kinds of pedagogy should be adopted to promote an enterprise culture in schools and in classrooms.

Deuchar's own research involved ten primary schools in Scotland. His aim was to find out the perceptions of teachers and headteachers of enterprise, including the purpose and role of enterprise education. His focus was also on the links between enterprise and citizenship. The title of the relevant chapter in his book is taken from a quotation from an interview with a teacher in one of the schools:

'I think it is more about letting go the reins a bit as a teacher. I feel sometimes it's difficult for us to give the children real responsibility ...'

(p. 39)

This theme of giving the pupils more responsibility comes up time and time again in the literature about enterprise (as well as citizenship and, indeed, many of the other classrooms in this book). Another teacher uses words like 'forward-thinking', 'leadership skills' and 'work well with others', while terms like 'thoughtful', 'kind' and 'new ideas' and 'confidence' came up in discussions with other teachers. Deuchar uses the term 'social responsibility' to sum up teachers' views of the kinds of behaviours and attitudes they hoped that enterprise education would inculcate among young people (p. 40). Clearly these have implications for pedagogy. Teachers tended to describe teaching styles which were less didactic and more collaborative than in some other areas of the curriculum.

When it came to teachers' perceptions of the desired outcomes of enterprise education, there was a mix of views. Some emphasised 'developing pupils' knowledge and understanding of the nature of business' while others talked about 'skills' including 'problem-solving, working and communicating with others' (p. 41). Some advocated a 'change of approach away from enterprise education to the education of children to become enterprising people' (p. 41). For many teachers, enterprise was a way of motivating pupils seen as 'low achievers' (p. 42) and others suggested that there was a transfer of skills to other aspects of the curriculum. In general, teachers talked of gains in 'confidence and maturity' especially among 'less academically able pupils'. The most common negative comment was the pressure of a 'crowded curriculum' (p. 42) and the pressure of attainment targets, externally imposed.

The tensions reported by teachers are not unique to this aspect of the school experience of course, but given that enterprise could be seen as additional to the existing core curriculum, it is, therefore, more vulnerable. While one headteacher argued that 'enabling and empowering children is having a knock-on effect on attainment' and therefore helping the school meet its attainment targets (p. 42), the general view among the profession is that these are conflicting pressures and that, in the final analysis, attainment measures which are public and are used to measure the schools' effectiveness will tend to outweigh other considerations.

Enterprising approaches: a CPD approach

One Scottish Council, South Lanarkshire, has produced a CPD resource for schools which has sections on Developing Thinking, Learning Collaboratively, Assessment is for Learning, and Enterprising Approaches. The format is similar for each: one or two DVDs, produced by the Council itself (perhaps based on a one-day conference with a well-known speaker) or one produced nationally (by Learning and Teaching Scotland and/or the Scottish Executive Education Department); some background information; activities of a CPD nature to be done individually, in small groups or by a whole-school staff; materials which could be applied in the classroom or in the school; and additional reading.

---

1 **Introduction to Determined to Succeed (DtS): Enterprise in Education (p. 5)**
2 **What is Enterprise in Education? (p. 9)**
   • DtS DVD
   • Reflection and Activities
   • Further reading
3 **What are enterprising skills and attitudes? (p. 12)**
   • SLC DVD
   • Reflection and Activities
   • Further reading
4 **What are enterprising approaches to learning and teaching? (p. 15)**
   • DtS DVD
   • Reflection and activities
   • Further reading
5 **Ideas for introducing enterprise activities into the Curriculum (p. 18)**
   • SLC DVD
   • Reflection and Activities
   • Further reading
6 **Interdisciplinary activities (p. 22)**
   • Activity
   • Reflection
7 **What does an enterprising lesson look like? (p. 25)**
   • Further reading
   • Reflection

8 **Careers and the world of work** (p. 29)
   - DtS DVD
   - SLC DVD
   - Reflection and Activities
   - Further reading
9 **Why should enterprising approaches appeal to teachers?** (p. 33)
   - Reflection and Activity

(South Lanarkshire Council, 2007,
Contents Page, Section 3)

The most relevant section for our present purposes is number 7, the enterprising lesson. Here the writers use a flow-chart format to describe a 'model lesson'. Around the perimeter of the flow-chart are boxes with links to *A Curriculum for Excellence, Assessment is for Learning* and *Key Strategies of Enterprise Education*. The immediate reaction of many teachers may well be that this lesson format has generic elements – sharing learning intentions and success criteria with pupils; linking lesson content with other learning; a variety of activities, determined by the outcomes; strategies to be used by teachers to promote thinking; self- and peer-assessment; next steps; and, finally, use of resources.

The overlaps between enterprise and a number of the other foci explored in this book are stark. In this Local Authority CPD resource, the message is clear: the initiatives which are being promoted to Scottish teachers do not – cannot – be done in isolation from one another. Indeed, the final section of the pack asks the question 'Why should enterprising approaches appeal to teachers?', and the Activity asks teachers to make connections between an enterprising approach and Assessment is for Learning, Learning Collaboratively and Thinking Skills (the other sections in the CPD pack).

Principles of the enterprising classroom

- *A can-do attitude*   For too many pupils, failure is a barrier, something to be avoided at all costs. Trying something new is a risky endeavour; when failure is experienced, the first thought is to give up. The root of this attitude may be a lack of encouragement in the past, humiliation when failure was made public or simply a lack of self-belief. If, on the other hand, the pupil is aware of the role of failure in learning, understands that nothing that is worthwhile can be learned without some failure along the way, that, indeed, failure is an opportunity, not a problem, then can-do can replace won't-try as the dominant culture of the classroom.

- *Empowering the learner*   The learning process for most pupils is not something which needs to be considered. The teacher says 'learn this for tomorrow' or 'learn this for homework' and the pupils do it (or not, as the case may be). If a pupil were to say to the teacher one day 'Miss/Sir, could you expand on your use of the word "learn" in this context?' or 'Miss/Sir, do you wish the learning to be deep or superficial; will it be enough to locate the learning in my short-term memory or would you wish me to be able to apply this learning to new and unforeseen contexts?', what would be the teacher's reaction; annoyance, alarm, amusement, anger, outrage or happiness?

- *Problem-solving*   The enterprising classroom is one where real problems, affecting pupils and their communities, will be used as the context for learning. Whether it is a three-year project to improve the health and wellbeing of the community (an example of a *rich task* from the Queensland approach (OCE, 2005)) or having to build a bridge strong enough to enable the pupils to cross it using only a limited range of materials, the aim will be to get pupils to see problems as their friends. The tougher the problem, the more creative the solution. And problem-solving skills are not always highly correlated with academic learning, so all pupils start from an equal footing and have an equal chance of success.

POINTS FOR REFLECTION

1 Enterprise has become a big issue in schools in recent years. What do you think it can contribute to the education process? Can you see any pitfalls?

2 What is your view of the advice and CPD offered within Determined to Succeed?

3 What do you think of the principles of *the enterprising classroom?*

8 The classroom without limits

> At the Gorge of Lu, the great waterfall plunges for thousands of feet, its spray visible for miles. In the churning waters below, no living creature can be seen. One day, K'ung Fu-tse was standing at a distance from the water's edge, when he saw an old man being tossed about in the turbulent water. He called to his disciples, and together they ran to rescue the victim. By the time they reached the water, the old man had climbed out onto the bank and was walking along, smiling to himself.
>
> K'ung Fu-tse hurried up to him. 'You would have to be a ghost to survive that,' he said, 'but you seem to be a man, instead. What secret power do you have?' 'Nothing special,' the old man replied. 'I began to learn when I was very young, and grew up practising it. Now I am certain of success. I go down with the water and come up with the water. I follow it and forget myself. I survive because I don't struggle against the water's superior power. That's all.'
>
> **Benjamin Hoff, *The Tao of Pooh***

Preamble

The issue of 'setting' pupils into classes on the basis of an assessment of their attainment through a test or examination has a long history, dating back to the days when the ideas of the psychometricians held sway in education. In the late nineteenth and early twentieth centuries, the idea that there was a single thing called intelligence became current. It was believed that it could be measured (in a scientific age, everything could be measured) but more importantly it could provide a scientific basis for selection in education. Not only could it provide a basis (through the 11+ or the Qualifying Examination) for selection between academic and non-academic secondary schools, but once the pupils were in their designated school, they could be more finely selected (streaming or setting) into classes according to some measure of their ability.

Feuerstein *et al.* (2002) have written about the 'Effect of Homogeneous Grouping' suggesting that 'serious doubt can be raised concerning all of the assumptions and predictions underlying the practice of homogeneous ability grouping' (p. 20). They quote from Findley and Bryan:

> The effect of grouping procedures ... is generally to put low achievers of all kinds together and to deprive them of stimulation of middle-class children as learning models and helpers.
>
> (p. 21)

Indeed, Feuerstein *et al.* observe that 'homogeneity creates a status quo' (p. 21).

Drawing on research in Scotland (Smith and Sutherland, 2006; Boyd, 2007) and England (Hallam and Ireson, 2005; Kutnick *et al.*, 2005), will offer a critique of the principle of selection, internal or external. The growing body of research evidence against the use of setting as a means of raising attainment, it will be argued, is well nigh overwhelming. Nevertheless, its appeal to teachers remains secure and the reasons for this phenomenon will be explored.

In particular the concept of 'learning without limits' (Hart *et al.*, 2004) will be considered. The key issue of how teachers can make the learning in their classrooms accessible to all pupils, irrespective of their prior attainment, is addressed in a series of case studies in Hart *et al.* (2004). In this chapter, the implications of *A Curriculum for Excellence* for the practice of setting will be explored.

Selection – the default position?

The present author's first taste of decision-making came in a most unexpected way. It was towards the end of my first year of teaching in a junior secondary school. In 1971, selection by ability was still practised, notwithstanding the fact that six years earlier the then Labour Government had introduced legislation to create non-selective comprehensive schools. Selection took place at the end of primary school by means of the Qualifying Exam ('the 'quali'), known as the 11+ in other parts of the United Kingdom, and so the pupils in this school were part of the 65% or so of the pupil population considered to be 'non-academic'. However, the Local Authority in which the school was situated was moving gradually towards comprehensivisation, and the school was to have its first comprehensive, non-selective intake at the beginning of the next school year in August 1971. Thus, our final staff meeting of session 1970/71 took place in classroom and the agenda was devoted to final preparations for the new, comprehensive S1 to be accommodated in the new building which would soon house the whole of the new school. The headteacher, a man not noted for his curricular perspicacity, introduced the item headed 'class organisation':

'Right, the new First Year', he announced, 'how will we organise the classes?'

There was a silence. Nervously, I raised my hand.

'Brian', he said, 'what do you think?'

I was already a supporter of the comprehensive principle and I agreed with equality of opportunity. I had read T. S. Eliot's *Notes Towards a Definition of Culture* (1948) where he suggested that 'the function of schooling is to preserve the class and select the elite' and had been appalled. So, tentatively, I replied,

'I think they should be mixed ability.'

'OK. What do others think?' asked the headteacher.

There was no further suggestion.

'Right; mixed ability it is', and he moved on to the next item on the agenda!

Class organisation: what can research tell us?

Of all the justifications advanced for setting, the appeal to common sense is perhaps the most insidious. It suggests that some children simply have more ability, or intelligence, than others; that this is more or less fixed and measurable by tests; and that we can predict with some certainty how children will learn as a result. This is the common-sense view of the world.

But, as professionals, we surely have to examine such views and challenge them when we have evidence to do so. We have challenged, in my professional lifetime, similarly dubious views on gender, race and social class, though in some of these cases the struggle still goes on. Common sense can spawn very persistent myths.

Of course, the setting debate is not new. In the 1960s, opposition to the selection of pupils based on ability was so widespread among professionals and politicians of all parties that comprehensive education and the concept of mixed-ability teaching were introduced to ensure that no child had limits placed on their potential to learn successfully. My first appointment was in a junior secondary where I saw at first hand the consequences of selection by ability. By the time pupils had been placed in 3m2(boys), they had got the message that they were 'thick'.

So why, after four decades of comprehensive education, during which time Scottish teachers have become familiar with theories of intelligence which challenge the notion that some children are thick, are we still having this debate? We can safely assume that no headteacher or head of department would introduce setting deliberately to harm pupils. Presumably, the motivation for this practice stems from this common-sense belief that some pupils are more able and others less able, and that these two groups cannot learn together.

Surely, as professionals, we have a duty to engage with these issues in an informed discussion based on evidence? In Scotland the issue of class organisation has been prominent since the 1990s when HMI(E) began to advocate the practice of setting pupils by prior attainment as a strategy for raising attainment. A literature review undertaken by Harlen and Malcolm was published in 1997, a year after the report it had been commissioned by HMI to inform. Its conclusions did not support the advice given to schools by HMI. Boyd (2005) has outlined the recent history of the setting versus mixed ability debate in Scotland, while the most comprehensive treatment of the issues of intelligence, ability and potential has been provided by Hart *et al.* (2004). In Scotland, Smith and Sutherland (2006) have published accounts of pupil perceptions on setting, while the American Adam Gamoran has written extensively on setting in Scotland and 'tracking' in America. Class organisation and organisation of learners within classes clearly has direct influence on pupil achievement, and decisions made by schools and departments on this matter should only be made after full consideration of the evidence available.

A Scottish Case study

The present writer (Boyd, 2007) was asked by a Scottish Local Authority to speak to a number of Principal Teachers (PTs) of English who had asked permission to deviate from the policy of having mixed-ability classes in S1 and S2. They felt under pressure, some from colleagues within the department, some from Senior Management Teams, to improve their results (in this case, the number of pupils achieving Levels E and F within the 5–14 Programme). At a meeting where the research evidence on setting and mixed ability was considered, one PT summed up the views of his colleagues: 'mixed-ability teaching is just too hard'. It was agreed that each of the departments would be visited for a morning. Classes would be observed, pupils interviewed and a departmental meeting attended to discuss the issues surrounding class organisation. In those schools which had already moved to setting in S2 (in contravention of the Local Authority's policy), what they had done was to take the top seven or so pupils from each S1 class and created a 'Level F' class. These classes were visited and the pupils asked how they liked being in this class. In general, the views were positive; teachers and pupils liked it. Pupils liked the fact that there were fewer distractions from pupils who were poorly motivated, they liked their relationship with the teacher, they liked the fact that they would not be thought a 'swot' if they answered a question in class. But some also felt that the pace was now too fast and that there were other pupils who could have been in the top set but weren't. One school had carried out a survey of pupils' views on setting, and the results indicated that not only do pupils have insightful views on these (and most other) issues, but they can see the complexities of the situation: that some pupils gain while others lose out.

Most telling of all were the visits to the lower sets in S2 in those same schools. Here, the work rate was noticeably slower, the behaviour was more difficult, time on task less and the overall classroom climate much less congenial than in the top sets. But, most importantly, in discussion with teachers later in departmental meetings, there was a strong view that these S2 sets were much less effective than the S1 classes the previous year. In other words, the success of the S1 mixed-ability classes had been sacrificed in order to create top sets who would, it was hoped, not only achieve Level F but go on to achieve A passes at Higher, some four years on. In one school, the open discussion at this meeting resulted in a change of policy; in others, the discussion about class organisation continued. In one school, the department was convinced that mixed ability was the best way of organising classes, but the Senior Management Team was applying pressure for change.

The article in which this case study is described concludes with a number of reflections which highlight some of the paradoxes which setting produces:

1 The quality of learning and teaching in S1 mixed ability classes observed was high. So too was that in top S2 sets. In other S2 sets, it was more variable.

2 The departments which set in S2 do so mainly for reasons linked to raising attainment as measured by 5–14 Levels, especially Levels E and F.

3 The effect of setting in S2 on the lower sets is, in the main, negative from the teachers' point of view. Pupils have more mixed views.

4 The effect of setting on top sets is positive from teachers' and pupils' perspectives.

5 The added effect of reduction in class size in one school seemed to ameliorate the situation somewhat in the broad-banded sets (though there was some variation from class to class).

6 The advantages most often cited for creating top sets, including high levels of motivation, challenge of more able learners, brisk pace of work and appropriate resources, were not confined to top sets but were also observable in S1 mixed ability classes in most of the schools visited.

7 Setting by attainment creates a gender imbalance unless the school/department intervenes positively to prevent it.

(Boyd, 2007, p. 292)

Class organisation and pedagogy

Looking at Mathematics in S2, Boaler *et al.* (2000) concentrated on:

- the relationship between pedagogy and the set being taught
- the views of pupils in sets
- the efficacy of setting as a means of improving pupil attainment.

They found that teachers who had both mixed-ability and set classes changed their pedagogy from one to the other. Most pupils in lower sets were 'unhappy with their placement'. Boaler *et al.* coined the phrase 'curriculum polarisation' to describe the 'restriction of opportunity to learn for students in lower sets, and students in top sets being required to learn at a pace which was, for many students, incompatible with understanding'.

Two of the most prolific writers in recent years on the subject of setting have been Susan Hallam and Judith Ireson, of London University. In 2005, they set out to compare secondary school teachers' 'pedagogical practices' when working with mixed-ability and ability-grouped classes. Their findings echoed those of Boaler *et al.*, with teachers who taught both mixed-ability and ability-grouped classes suggesting that their pedagogy changed according to the composition of the class being taught. On one level, this seems unremarkable: of course teachers' styles must change according to the class in front of them. However, this study suggests that teachers were forced into these changes because the nature of the set (high, low, average) did not allow them to teach in the ways in which they wished.

Setting and pupil attitude and self-concept

In 2001, Ireson, Hallam and Plewis looked at the effects of setting on pupils' 'self-concept'. They found that pupils' self-concept was highest in schools using 'moderate levels of setting'. Hallam and Ireson's 2006 study explored pupils' preferences for particular types of grouping practices. In contrast with the Boaler study, they reported that 'the majority of pupils preferred setting', and that the pupils' main reason was that it 'enabled work to be matched to learning needs'. The authors concluded that if this is the key issue then there may be ways other than setting in which it could be achieved.

Class organisation and attainment

Of all the arguments advanced in favour of setting, raising attainment is by far the most common and most compelling for politicians and curriculum managers. In 2005, Ireson, Hallam and Hurley looked at whether setting improves attainment in English, Mathematics or Science. They concluded that there 'were no significant effects of setting' on attainment. Any effects they did find were not consistent across the subjects or across higher- and lower-attaining pupils. In addition, students of similar prior attainment consistently scored better when in higher sets. Gender and socio-economic status were also associated with lower attainment.

Previously, Ireson, Clark and Hallam (2002) had studied over 6,000 students in English secondary schools. The study found that, when other variables were controlled, the number of years of setting had virtually no effect on average GCSE attainment. Yet there was a profound effect on the attainment of individual students of the same ability who were placed in higher or lower sets.

Class organisation and pupil grouping

In two major literature reviews, Kutnick et al. (2005) looked at the effects of pupil grouping and concluded that the debate on pupil grouping is often polarised. They singled out *within-class grouping* as an important but neglected area for research. They concluded that no one form of grouping benefits all pupils. They suggest that within-class groupings, if coupled with personalisation of learning, may have the potential to overcome some of the barriers to learning which some pupils face.

When setting is used, Kutnick et al. suggest that there is less movement among sets than might be expected. They found that boys, pupils from ethnic minority backgrounds and those with special educational needs are over-represented in lower sets, and lower-achieving pupils appear to have their progress limited in lower sets in Maths. They recommend that when schools are making decisions about pupil grouping, they should examine the evidence, be flexible and adaptable and examine the effects of their policies in this area. They make a case for within-class groupings, sensitively organised, and suggest that a greater 'focus on pedagogy' (p. 4) would be beneficial.

Class organisation and socio-economic status (SES)

In *The Urban Primary School*, McGuire *et al.* (2006) look at the thorny issue of social class and ability setting. They argue that we cannot ignore the fact that, when ability setting is used, the lowest sets have the highest concentration of pupils from areas of disadvantage. This simply reinforces evidence from four decades of school effectiveness research from across the world, including Scotland (MacBeath and Mortimore, 2001). The practice of setting by ability is not inclusive, argue the authors, and they suggest that what is needed is 'a political commitment to eradicate social inequalities and injustices in education'. While the focus of the research is on the primary school, the conclusions have a resonance across the sectors.

Class organisation and pupil perspectives

In the real-life schools setting, the group which rarely gets consulted is the pupils themselves. Dylan Wiliam and colleagues from Kings College in London did just this in the late 1990s and found that pupils in top Maths sets reported that they felt stressed, that they enjoyed the subject less because of the heavy emphasis on exam-based work and often felt guilty that friends had not got into the top set when they felt they were equally able at Maths. More recently, Chris Smith and Margaret Sutherland at the University of Glasgow have also reported concerns among young people about the practice of setting. When *Tell Them from Me* was written in 1980 by Gow and McPherson, it reminded us that the pupil voice needs to be heard when we as professionals make decisions which might affect their life chances.

Class organisation and equality of opportunity

In a small-scale study, Alison Barker (2003) compared two Year 9 (S3) classes, one mixed ability and one set, in terms of the opportunities each received in preparation for their SATs. She found that, in low sets, 'students' potential is repeatedly limited by low expectations of teachers ...' (p. 13) She concedes that 'planning and delivering a genuinely differentiated curriculum for mixed ability classes is harder than teaching top, middle or bottoms sets' (p. 13) but maintains a commitment to mixed-ability teaching on the basis that the evidence for setting as a means of raising attainment is flimsy.

Learning without limits

A significant contribution to this area of study is *Learning without Limits* (Hart *et al.*, 2004). The authors drew on a number of case studies of teachers who had responded to an advertisement as having 'rejected ability labelling and ... developed successful practices consistent with their ideas' (pp. 44–45), and examined the literature on intelligence and achievement. The result is a powerful case for 'an alternative improvement agenda' (p. 244). They conclude that what is required is a pedagogy which transcends labels and categories of pupils based on tests or examinations. In suggesting 'an alternative template' (p. 245) they acknowledge that it may require 'a [more] profound shift in thinking' and suggest ways in which a move from an 'ability mindset' to a 'transformability mindset' (p. 247) might be made. In a helpful final chapter, they make connections among their ideas and some core theoretical ideas and they conclude that '... in teaching for transformability, "good practice" is not just about what teachers *do,* but also what they do *not* do' (p. 263). Included in these latter practices are 'sorting pupils (in their mind or in practice) into ability groups and differentiating teaching (expectations, tasks, content, questions, interactions, feedback on work) on the basis of such arrangements' (p. 263).

The book provides not just a comprehensive review of the ways in which views of intelligence have limited our expectations of young people's capability to learn; it also gives evidence of teachers in every sector who choose to teach pupils in mixed-ability classes and who so do with creativity, with commitment and with success. There are nine teachers featured in the book, four who taught in primary schools and five in secondary. The primary classes featured ranged from Year 1 (P2) to a composite Year 5 and 6 (P6 and 7) and the secondary subjects included were three English, one Maths and one Humanities, ranging from Year 9 (S3) to Year 11 (S5). The descriptions are those of the researchers, based on lesson observation and on 'many hours' of interviews and group discussion (p. 57).

The nine vignettes of teachers' practice are compelling; these are people whose commitment to teaching *without limits* manifests itself in different ways. It is not appropriate here to look in detail at all nine teachers; two will suffice, one from primary and one from secondary. Anne, with her Year 1 class, works on a model which the researchers feel is similar to that set out by Dewey in 1899 where the school is at the centre but it reaches out to:

- the home
- the garden, the park, the country, the world
- the university, laboratories, museums and libraries
- business and the needs and forces of industry.

Anne is described as 'to some degree out of step with some of her colleagues' in that she says 'I want them to *think*' and 'I honestly think they'll learn to spell when they get older' (p. 63). She is described as 'in no sense an out-and-out rebel' (p. 63) but she clearly has the courage to think in unconventional ways. Her planning is rigorous but she is prepared to deviate from it; her classroom is structured but she is prepared to be flexible. Anne's commitment to teaching without limits had a personal element to it. Her daughter, who graduated with a first class degree, had been 'stuck in a bottom set' in school and the family had to rally round to support her and allow her to demonstrate her potential to learn. All-in-all, she is determined that every child is seen as having the potential to be a successful learner, even if it means going outside the limits of the plan, the classroom or even the school itself.

Yahi's experience of Maths learning was one of 'rote learning, dictation, memorizing, repetition' (p. 128) and, undoubtedly part of his own approach to teaching the subject is based on his desire not to 'put them through that'. Part of his approach is geared towards combating that element of youth culture which does not see learning as 'cool'. He has decided not to tackle it head on with his Year 10 class but rather to try to engage their curiosity. His first step is to make his classroom attractive, stimulating and lively, with displays of problems, designs and patterns which catch the pupils' interest. The school sets for Maths, and Yahi's is a 'middle' set. He has decided that his lessons need to have a pattern or rhythm; there is a moment's quiet reflection at the start and a five-minute break in the middle, both designed to promote greater relaxation and concentration. He is very conscious of the 'emotional dimension of learning' (p. 131) and regularly asks pupils to give written feedback on how the term has gone. He uses friendship groupings within the class but also at times gets people who don't know each other well to work together. For him, building confidence and trust is at the heart of teaching *without limits,* and one measure of this is the frequency with which the pupils ask questions. All of this is within the framework of class rules, negotiated with the pupils, which emphasise punctuality, hard work and positive behaviour. Crucially, he says, 'I think my expectations are very high – and I think they need to know this' (p. 136). Challenge and support are at the heart of his philosophy.

Setting versus mixed ability *should* be yesterday's debate. Tomorrow's debate is about freeing up teachers and others to work with young people in creative and innovative ways so that they can develop as successful learners, confident individuals, effective contributors and responsible citizens.

The way forward may be to focus on the learning process and the factors which promote and hinder it. We need to continue to look critically at ideas and approaches to learning and teaching which render setting obsolete. Already, schools and local authorities are doing just that, whether it is cooperative learning, thinking skills or dialogic teaching. We know that too many young people underachieve, particularly in areas of social disadvantage, but it is not, as common sense might suggest, because they are 'less able' than their contemporaries. Setting does not promote successful learning; good teaching does.

Principles of the classroom without limits

The classroom without limits will embody the following principles:

- *No labels* There is a temptation to use convenient labels as a short hand. If a teacher says 'I've got my Foundies next period' is s/he simply using an economical form of language derived from one of the three levels of Standard Grade achievement (Foundation, General and Credit), or is it an insidious, albeit possibly unintentional, form of labelling? If a teacher refers to her 'Level B group', is it simply descriptive or does it suggest that certain (low) expectations are at play? Is it ever legitimate to transfer an epithet in this context; using a word or a letter which describes a level of attainment to describe a human being?

- *Pupils are grouped for specific purposes* The composition of the group in the classroom without limits will be linked to the nature of the task and the kinds of experience, expertise, interests, skills and dispositions of the pupils. If the task is a problem-solving one requiring a mix of intelligence, knowledge, creativity and practical application, it is unlikely that the four or five pupils who score highest in some proxy measure of IQ will be the group most likely to succeed.

- *Teachers are confident in their own creativity* There is a real sense in which teaching is about taking risks, without being reckless. Teachers from time immemorial have tried new things, tried new ways of doing old things and, in Perkins' words, have tried to 'wild the tame'. Finding creative ways of thinking about the world, of encouraging pupils to take new perspectives and of challenging them to think differently, are all parts of a good teacher's repertoire. Over the last 25 years or more, there has been scant reward in the system for being creative; getting pupils through exams successfully has been seen as the most important thing to do. Now teachers need to be given the confidence to be creative and to believe that in so doing they will enable their pupils to achieve greater success, in life as well as in exams.

POINTS FOR REFLECTION

1. The practice of organising pupils into classes within secondary (or into cross-stage groups in primary) is often called *setting*. What are the advantages and disadvantages in your view?

2. If the research evidence is so strongly against the practice of setting, why does it continue to be the 'default position' in schools?

3. Does the 'Learning without Limits' approach have any attractions for you?

4. What do you think of the principles of *the classroom without limits*?

9 The cooperative classroom

> 'Well,' said the Owl, 'the customary procedure in such cases is as follows.' 'What does Crustimoney Proseedcake mean?' said Pooh. 'For I am a bear of Very Little Brain, and long words Bother me.' 'It means the Things to Do.' 'As long as it means that, I don't mind,' said Pooh humbly.
>
> **Benjamin Hoff, *The Tao of Pooh***

Learning: a solitary or a cooperative activity?

If we were to look inside the classrooms of many traditional schools, it would appear that silence and solitary endeavour were the hallmarks of the learning classroom. Talk was associated with noise, noise with indiscipline. Cooperation was considered to be cheating, and single desks, placed just far enough away from one another so that no pupil could see another's work, were the furniture of choice. Even when double desks were introduced, they did not herald a shift to cooperative learning; they simply meant that teachers had to be more vigilant.

Even when talk did take place, it was rarely *dialogue*. More often than not, the teacher talked and the pupils listened. Whether they understood or not was a moot point, and, often, it was not until the end-of-term test that the teacher found out if understanding had taken place, and by then, for some, it was too late. For many learners, the misunderstanding took place *because* of the teacher-talk, not *despite* it. Like Pooh, they simply could not fathom the impenetrable depths of the teacher's language. As one pupil said to the present author early in his career, 'Sir, you talk like a book'!

In this chapter we consider the concept of learning as a social activity. We look briefly at the work of, arguably, the most influential educational theorist of the twentieth century, Lev Vygotsky, and consider three major programmes or approaches based on his work:

- dialogic teaching
- cooperative learning
- critical skills.

All three have been around for some time, the first in England, the second in Canada and the third in the United States. They have all made their way to Scotland since the late 1990s and have attracted an enthusiastic following. However, the function of a theory is not to command allegiance, rather it is to help to clarify and illuminate ideas and practices. The aim here, therefore, is not to choose among these approaches, all of which share a common lineage, but to look at the principles on which they are based, the claims they make for their success and what they have to offer the Scottish classroom teacher.

Vygotsky in the modern classroom

Kozulin (1994) has written about 'creating powerful thinkers in teachers and students'. He explores the relationships between Vygotsky's 'spontaneous' and 'scientific' concepts. The former 'emerge from the child's own reflections on everyday experiences; they are rich but unsystematic and highly contextual' (p. 278).

On the other hand, 'scientific' concepts 'originate in the structured and specialised activity of classroom instruction and are characterised by systematic and logical organisation' (p. 278). What is important to note here is that the 'scientific' concepts do not necessarily relate to science itself; it is the organisation of the concepts, their structure, which is scientific. While Piaget argued that conceptual learning could only begin when a certain developmental level was reached, Vygotsky saw the classroom as a place where more structured learning 'itself promotes cognitive development' (p. 278).

This analysis of Vygotsky's theory is helpful because it leads to what Kozulin calls 'the principle of collectively distributed problem solving' (p. 283). His description of the method is similar to that proposed more recently as part of Assessment is for Learning: 'jigsawing'. He suggests that by presenting the task so that different groups within the class look at different 'segments' of the problem, the interpersonal contact becomes a 'means for achieving the goals of learning' (p. 283). The role of the teacher changes in this context. It becomes one of 'advisor and participant' or 'senior member' of the scientific group. Feuerstein (1990) has elaborated Vygotsky's theory and has suggested that the teacher becomes a 'mediator' of the child's learning, in the same way that thoughtful parents use everyday experiences to create opportunities for generalised learning.

For the modern classroom, the key message of Feuerstein is that the teacher and the peer group can mediate learning in ways which enable the learner to create the 'cognitive prerequisites that make direct learning effective'. If these prerequisites are not present in the child for whatever reason, argues Feuerstein, then the Piagetian stages will not occur nor will the child benefit from the introduction of a Vygotskian psychological tool. The key additional element is mediation. For Feuerstein, the mediation of 'an adult or more competent peer is the necessary condition for the establishment of cognitive prerequisites indispensable for the child's further learning' (Kozulin, 1994, p. 285).

The importance of this brief theoretical introduction to cooperative learning will become apparent as we consider three of the most important programmes in use in Scottish schools at present. Each of them makes specific reference to a Vygotskian perspective but they each focus differently on elements of the learning process and how it can be supported in the classroom.

Dialogic teaching

Professor Robin Alexander's work, *Towards Dialogic teaching: Rethinking Classroom Talk* (2006) 'presents the case for dialogic teaching as not another transient educational fad'. This 57-page A5 booklet sets out the principles, classroom indicators to guide professional practice, the research base and further reading. Alexander's work starts from the premise that 'Talk has always been one of the essential tools of teaching' and he has described dialogic teaching as 'an "emerging pedagogy" of the spoken word' (p. 9).

Alexander's work draws on a major international research study in which he has been involved since 1992. In his keynote lecture to the national conference of the International Association for Cognitive Education and Psychology in 2005, entitled 'Culture, dialogue and learning', he makes a powerful case for talk being a central part of pedagogy (defined as 'the act of teaching together with the ideas, values and collective histories which inform, shape and explain that act'). He argues that talk, of all the tools available to the teacher, is 'the most pervasive in its use and powerful in its possibilities', but this use of talk is 'much less common than it should be' in classrooms. He suggests that the most pervasive use of talk is the '"recitation script" of closed teacher questions, brief recall answers and minimal feedback' (p. 2) and quotes Nystrand et al. (1997) who suggest that 'When recitation starts, remembering and guessing supplant thinking' (p. 6). Interestingly, Alexander also warns against too many unfocused open questions, which can be unchallenging and may be accompanied by praise rather than meaningful feedback. He suggests that the dialogue which ought to take place in classrooms has two clear functions: to enable pupils to 'learn about the world' and teachers to 'learn about children' (p. 3).

Alexander, in his various publications, has developed a set of *principles* of dialogic teaching:

> *Collective:* teachers and children address learning tasks together, whether as a group or as a class, rather than in isolation;
> *Reciprocal:* teachers and children listen to each other, share ideas and consider alternative viewpoints;
> *Supportive:* children articulate their ideas freely, without fear of embarrassment over 'wrong' answers; and they help each other to reach common understandings;
> *Cumulative:* teachers and children build on their own and others' ideas and chain them into coherent lines of thinking and enquiry;
> *Purposeful:* teachers plan and facilitate dialogic teaching with particular educational goals in view.
>
> (Alexander, 2005, p. 26)

Alexander makes explicit the link between his two favoured repertoires of *discussion* and *dialogue* and what he calls the 'core skills of citizenship' (2005, p. 31). His thesis is that a society in which talk is at the heart of the learning and teaching process is one in which its citizens will be able to hold to account its decision-makers. Alexander offers a detailed list of repertoires of *learning talk* and *organisational contexts*. Among the former, he lists many activities which crop up in typologies of thinking skills, such as *analyse and solve problems, speculate and imagine, explore and evaluate ideas* and *argue, reason and justify*. He gives advice on pupil behaviours which will facilitate these repertoires, namely, *listen, be receptive to alternative viewpoints, think aloud about what they hear* and *give others time to think*.

He lists five 'main ways of organising interaction':

- Whole-class teaching (teacher and class)
- Collective group work (teacher led)
- Collaborative group work (pupil led)
- One-to-one (teacher and pupil)
- One-to-one (pupil pairs)

(p. 35)

He then offers four pages of bullet-pointed suggestions on when dialogic teaching is 'facilitated and supported'.

In *Culture, dialogue and learning* (2005), Alexander outlined some of the challenges he and his fellow researchers were facing in British classrooms. He suggests that there is a growing gap between the small number of teachers 'who are achieving real change and those whose interaction has shifted rather less' (p. 15). The quality of feedback given by teachers, he argues, is still often 'minimal and judgemental ... rather than informative' (p. 15). He also distinguishes between 'teacher talk' and 'learning talk' and suggests that there still is not enough of the latter. In addition, he re-iterates that 'recitation remains the default teaching mode' (p. 15). Finally, he raises perhaps the most challenging issue of all, his principle of *cumulative* talk, which demands that the teacher is able to use dialogue to extend the learner's understanding of the content of the learning, challenging, scaffolding and taking the learner's thinking forward (p. 16).

He concludes that his principles might usefully be divided into two groupings. He suggests that teachers might concentrate on the *ethos* and *dynamics* of the classroom with a view to making talk *collective, reciprocal and supportive*. Thereafter, by concentrating on the *purpose* and *content* of the talk, and by focusing on the *feedback*, the teachers can begin to consider how 'ideas can not merely be *exchanged* in an encouraging and supportive climate but also *built upon*' (2005, p. 16).

In his most recent edition of *Towards Dialogic Teaching* (2006), Alexander has a section entitled 'Learning to talk, talking to learn' (pp. 10–13) in which he looks at the evidence from psychology and neuroscience. He suggests that recent advances in neuroscience have indicated that 'talk is necessary not just for learning but also for the building of the brain itself' (p. 12). He quotes Goswami who, in turn, reinforces the Vygotskian view that 'higher order cognitive activities of the kind that characterise formal schooling require both conscious effort and direct intervention' (Alexander, 2006, p. 13). In other words, the role of the teacher as 'mediator' of learning is crucial. Alexander uses this new evidence to reinforce his contention that:

> ... the dynamics of talk matter no less than its content, while social and cognitive purposes go hand in hand.
>
> (Alexander, 2006, p. 13)

Towards Dialogic Teaching is an approach that is well-grounded in theory and in research, rigorous and demanding but capable of being understood and implemented by teachers in their classrooms. There is no doubt that Alexander is concerned that his approach is sometimes used by teachers in ways which do not transform their pedagogy as thoroughly as he would wish. He is critical of the persistence of 'recitation' in classrooms, of 'test' questions which do not promote thinking or dialogue, and of teachers dominating discussion. As with every approach or programme, there can be a gap between the purist view of its author and the more pragmatic, eclectic approach of teachers in the classroom. Even when dialogic teaching has been implemented only partially (in the view of Alexander), there is, nevertheless, evidence of real improvement in young people's learning, as the experience in Inverclyde demonstrates.

'Talking round corners': a case study – Inverclyde Council

In 2005, six primary schools in Inverclyde embarked on a project based on the work of Robin Alexander. The original intention was that it would be a small, pilot project, focusing on P6 and P7. In the event, as often happens with initiatives of this kind, more schools asked, and were given permission, to become involved, and not all of the schools confined the project to P6 and P7.

The final evaluation report, *Talking, Listening and Learning in Inverclyde* (Boyd and Lawson, 2007) was based on classroom observation, interviews with teachers, pupils and senior managers, and a pre- and post-project teacher questionnaire. The evaluation was largely qualitative in nature. In the timescale, there was no opportunity to test pupil 'attainment' in any formal sense. Rather, the aim was to look at discussion and dialogue, pupils' engagement in learning cooperatively, the role of the teacher in scaffolding learning and teachers' perceptions of the CPD process itself.

Both the interim and final reports made use of verbatim reports from participants to illustrate the findings, and, as is often the case in such evaluations, the pupils provided some gems:

> When the teacher asks a question and you put your hands up, someone gets picked and they say their answer. When you discuss it with your thumbs it goes in all sorts of different directions and you really think about it and understand it better. It's like talking round corners.
>
> (P7 pupil, Highlanders' Academy,
> quoted in Boyd and Lawson, 2007, p. 5)

This concept of 'talking round corners' is an interesting one. The pupil has clearly spotted what Alexander sees as one of the traditional practices used by teachers which actually *stifle* dialogue. The pupil has observed that, through dialogic teaching approaches, the discussion is less linear and more unpredictable, less teacher-dominated and more likely to lead to understanding. The evaluators reported that teachers had identified gains from using this approach:

Teachers identified many positive outcomes for pupils – both social and intellectual. The principal advantages identified were:

- enhanced pupil confidence and the realisation that it's OK to be wrong;
- sustained pupil engagement;
- greater degree of metacognition about, and reflection on, learning;
- improved discipline / self discipline;
- pupils with dyslexic type difficulties blossoming when they realise what they have to *say* is valued.
- improved vocabulary – early years pupils using words like 'joyless', 'glum', upper primary pupils talking about 'empathy';
- improved quality of writing across the curriculum;
- awareness of peers as a resource;
- much less teacher intervention – pupils much more willing to take responsibility for their own, and each other's, learning.

(pp. 6–7)

One of the challenges of such interim reports of initiatives only a year into their life is how to disentangle the effects which are the function of the novelty of a new approach from those which are likely to be lasting. The so-called Hawthorn Effect is well-known in psychology, giving rise to a concern that *any* new approach would have, albeit short term, a positive impact simply because of the novelty effect. It did not seem to the evaluators that this was the case in this project:

> The early evidence from the project so far is entirely positive. The Primary 1 and 2 classes provide a bonus which was not entirely unexpected, namely that the earlier this approach is embedded in the learning process the better. Our interim findings are that there are many examples of good practice.
>
> (p. 9)

However, it was important to find out whether, after another year, the same conclusions could be drawn.

The final report made use of DVD footage from a number of the schools. The project had grown a little between the dates of publication of the two reports, with other schools, including one for young people with moderate learning difficulties (MLD), now included. All of the original schools were still involved. CPD opportunities had continued and some schools had, unilaterally, disseminated the approach among their staff.

Interviews with teachers were positive, and what was interesting from a Scottish context was an understanding of the links to be made between the Talking, Listening and Learning (TLL) approach and other initiatives, from *A Curriculum for Excellence* to *Assessment is for Learning*. There was a recurring sense that dialogic teaching encouraged pupils to be better thinkers and therefore better learners and there were spin-offs such as improved concentration and behaviour, and less of a need to organise groups by similar levels of 'attainment':

> This teacher has recently moved to trios for group sessions but tries to mix them in terms of traditional judgements of 'ability'. She points out that the best readers and writers aren't necessarily the best in discussion.
>
> (p. 32)

Throughout the evaluation process, the pupils' views were sought. As one might expect, the older pupils were more able to reflect on their experiences and were often extremely insightful and articulate in their analysis of what they were doing, and why it helped them to be better learners.

Engaging with pupils on Talking, Listening and Learning in Inverclyde
Six pupils (3 P6 and 3 P7) met with the researcher in the Headteacher's room, unplanned, for around 30 minutes. Throughout the discussion, they used their skills and techniques developed by TLL. They put thumbs up or down, not in a demonstrative way, but patiently, naturally, as if that was the only civilised way of ensuring that everyone, including the researcher, got a turn. They articulated the principles and the practices of TLL. They talked about 'thinking' and its importance in learning. They discussed the concept of intelligences and how different pupils had different strengths. They understood the reason why it would be appropriate for a pupil with a good understanding of a topic [to] work with one who didn't and why both would benefit. They were aware of how difficult it might be for someone who did not understand to be asked, in front of the whole class, a question without being ready to answer it.

They explained the benefits of this approach to cooperative group discussion. They built on one another's comments, supported one another, took turns, challenged one another's ideas but in a non-critical way, and so on. They discussed with me the rationale for TLL, the importance of collaborative learning, the need to work with others who are less confident, the ethos of the classroom. They seemed to have internalised Vygotsky!

We discussed the challenges of transition to secondary. They were unsure whether secondary teachers would know about their work in the primary school, not just in the classroom but the way in which they ran assemblies, planning the content, introducing visiting speakers and giving votes of thanks. The confidence which working in this way had given them might or might not be acknowledged.

At the end, one of the P7 pupils, a 'sparky' boy with trendy, spiky hair spontaneously thanked the researcher on behalf of all the pupils (each of whom he referred to by name) for coming to talk to them and for taking an interest in their work.

(Boyd and Lawson, 2007, pp. 37–38)

The conclusion of the final evaluation report refers back to Professor Alexander's publication:

> Robin Alexander (2004) claims that '*dialogic teaching harnesses the power of talk to stimulate and develop pupils' thinking and advance their learning and understanding.*' (p. 5) The evidence from this project, albeit small-scale and of a relatively short duration, would tend to support his claim.
>
> (Boyd and Lawson, 2007, p.46)

Cooperative learning

The approach known as *cooperative learning* emerged from the work of Johnson and Johnson (1990) but is based on theory and research going back to Bruner, Vygotsky and others. In the introduction to their resource booklet *Cooperative Learning* (1999), Chris Ward and Jim Craigen, from the Durham District School Board, Ontario, Canada, define cooperative learning as 'the instructional use of small groups so that students work together to maximize their own and each other's learning' (p. 5). They argue that there is a 'positive interdependence among students' goal attainments' (p. 5) and suggest that in competitive situations 'there is a negative interdependence among goal achievements' (p. 5). They cite some 600 experimental studies and 100 correlational studies and claim that cooperation in learning results in:

> (a) higher achievement and greater productivity, (b) more caring, supportive and committed relationships, and (c) greater psychological health, social competence, and self-esteem.
>
> (Ward and Craigen, 1999, p. 6)

The authors, both experienced educators, are under no illusions about the ways in which pupils can become cooperative learners. They are clear that simply placing them in groups, around tables, and saying 'work together' won't do. They also concede that 'not all groups are cooperative' (p. 6). They argue that, if teachers wish their pupils to learn cooperatively, they must:

1 Take existing lessons, curricula and courses, and structure them cooperatively.
2 Tailor cooperative learning lessons to meet the unique instructional circumstances and needs of the curricula, subject areas and students.
3 Diagnose the problems some students may have in working together and intervene to increase the effectiveness of the student learning groups.

(p. 6)

They present a distinction between cooperative learning and traditional learning groups based on the work of Johnson, Johnson and Smith (1991):

Cooperative learning groups	Traditional learning groups
Positive interdependence	No interdependence
Individual accountability	No individual accountability
Heterogeneous membership	Homogeneous membership
Shared leadership	One appointed leader
Task and relationships emphasised	Only task emphasised
Social skills directly taught	Social skills assumed or ignored
Teacher monitors groups	Teacher ignores groups and intervenes
Group processing	No group processing

While these dichotomies seem a little stark at times (I can't imagine many teachers actually *ignoring* groups), nevertheless, many Scottish teachers will identify with some of the deficiencies of traditional group work, including the tendency towards 'ability grouping', the looseness of the group itself as a unit and the lack of accountability within the group for the work of individuals. However, it must also be said that many of the features of cooperative learning groups can be seen in Scottish classrooms, and that other initiatives have helped to focus on the nature of the process of cooperative learning, not least Assessment is for Learning and aspects of Citizenship and Determined to Succeed.

Ward and Craigen, in terms not dissimilar to *A Curriculum for Excellence*, and with echoes of David Perkins' (1992) notion of 'teaching for the unknown', offer a rationale for cooperative learning that begins from their assessment of the challenges of the twenty-first century. They suggest that transmission of knowledge may not be enough and that the skills required to solve problems cooperatively may be crucial in a rapidly changing world. They point to the increasingly pluralistic nature of society as justification for an emphasis on working together, and suggest that the process of learning is as important as the product. Learning to learn and developing learning strategies is what cooperative learning can facilitate, and, according to Johnson and Johnson (1990), it can also increase student achievement.

The booklet *Cooperative Learning* contains a section headed 'Role of the Teacher'. The advice given here is detailed and extensive, organised around four areas:

- make decisions
- set the lesson
- monitor and intervene
- evaluate and process.

Some of the advice fits well with other approaches, such as Specify Academic and Collaborative Objectives, Explain the Criteria for Success, Provide Task Assistance and Provide Closure. It also includes a section on 'Lesson Design: an advance organiser for the integration of pedagogy'. It is in this section that there is an attempt to move cooperative learning from social skills towards thinking skills and metacognition. The basic components of the design are:

- developing a mental set
- providing the information or input
- modelling or demonstrating key elements of the learning
- checking for understanding
- providing guided and independent practice
- bringing closure or extension to the learning.

Here, the links to other programmes and approaches seems clearer. The 'mental set' is similar to the 'understanding goal' (Perkins, 1995); the information or input is reminiscent of the 'cognitive conflict' (Adey and Shayer, 1994); modelling or demonstrating includes elements of Active Learning; checking for understanding is central to Teaching for Understanding, Assessment is for Learning, and Critical Skills; guided and independent practice has elements of peer- and/or self-assessment; and bringing closure is consolidation (Boyd and Simpson, 2000) and may have elements of understanding performances (Perkins, 1992).

What is clear from Ward and Craigen (1999) is that cooperative learning is a serious approach, well-grounded in educational theory and research, with an extensive range of practical classroom strategies to help teachers become confident and proficient. It does not shirk the controversies associated with cooperative learning (and with almost every other programme or approach to learning and teaching) and cites studies which support this pedagogy. Importantly, it has recently undergone an evaluation, funded by the then Scottish Executive Education Department (SEED), of its introduction into North Lanarkshire Council.

Critical Skills Programme – Education by design

'Education By Design', or the 'Critical Skills Programme' (www.networkcontinuum.co.uk) as it is known in Scotland, is a programme based on work developed in the United States and which has made a positive impact in a number of Scottish Local Authorities. Ably led by Colin Weatherly, a former secondary school headteacher, it has become an influential approach for the promotion of learning in primary and secondary schools.

The Level 1 Coaching Kit (Mobilia and Gordon, 1997) includes a section entitled 'Education by Design – What is it?', which offers four levels of understanding of the Critical Skills Programme. First, it is 'a set of tools and strategies for being purposeful in the process of engaging students in their learning'. It will help teachers organise their teaching, help students achieve their goals and 'focus on quality work' (p. 3). Second, it provides a 'framework for the design of a learning environment', using a 'process that honors democratic practices, collaborative work, and student responsibility for learning' (p. 3). Third, it is 'a model for transformational education'. It sees students and teachers as 'active collaborators' and represents a practical response to 'theoretical arguments supporting constructivist, collaborative, experiential, authentic and democratic learning environments' (p. 3). Finally, it is offered as a philosophy, a 'way of thinking'. It starts from the premise that learning is often 'messy' and suggests that 'with a well-designed learning environment, students and teachers can work together to assure the success of all' (p. 3).

This is a significant claim. It is based, not unlike A Curriculum for Excellence, on a set of values:

We believe that education must be experiential, must nurture interdependence, and must enable all members of each generation to develop the judgement necessary to take responsibility for:
the conduct of their lives,
the shaping of their societies,
and their participation in global issues.
We believe that judgement is the integration of knowledge, skills and standards of ethical behaviour that guides decisions, commitments and action.

(Mobilia and Gordon, 1997, p. 4)

Mobilia and Gordon look at the 'education by design' (EBD) classroom (the acronym EBD has been largely dropped for the UK context since it has another connotation: Emotional and Behavioural Difficulties) and list four 'foundational concepts' of the Critical Skills Programme:

• Experiential learning
• Collaborative learning communities
• Standards-driven learning
• Problem-based learning.

(p. 5)

However, it is the nine 'basic characteristics', and their detailed descriptors, which begin to bring the Critical Skills Programme to life:

1 Students frequently work as a team.
2 Students actively solve meaningful problems.
3 Students publicly exhibit their learning.
4 Students reflect on what they are learning and doing.
5 Students apply quality criteria to their work.
6 Teachers mediate, coach and support the learning process.
7 Targeted learning results guide culture, curriculum and assessment.
8 Work is interconnected.
9 Students take responsibility for and ownership of their learning and for the classroom community.

(p. 6)

Some of these characteristics are self-explanatory; however, a few merit some further explanation.

Students apply quality criteria to their work

There are, clearly, connections to be made here to the 'peer- and self-assessment' of Black and Wiliam's *Inside the Black Box* (1998). However, it is the emphasis on 'quality' which is a little different. These criteria, to be set at the beginning of a 'challenge', are a mix of teacher and student contributions and can apply to the product and the process of learning. They are designed to encourage students to 'raise their standard of excellence' and to help them 'discover what quality work is by providing models' (p. 9).

Targeted learning results guide culture, curriculum and assessment

This is an important perspective on the current attainment/achievement debate in Scotland. There are many educators who believe that externally imposed standards and targets, often linked to 'high stakes' examinations, stifle deep learning. This approach seeks to make any such targets transparent to the students thereby enabling them to incorporate the standards in their day-to-day classroom learning. It is not about narrowing the criteria for success, but about ensuring that if there are externally imposed standards then these should be known to the students and built into the process of problem-design, learning, de-briefing and self-assessment.

Students take responsibility for and ownership of their learning and for the classroom community

In many ways, this is the most powerful idea of all – the classroom as a 'learning community' (p. 11). Not only are students involved in setting goals and in decision-making as part of the learning process, but the whole class, teacher included, is a collaborative learning community. There is an interdependence and a sense of responsibility for the work of one another (similar to that within the group in cooperative learning). The highest expression of this is when pupils do not need teacher direction because they are in control of the work they need to do. 'Quality work' is the driving force, and the whole class has responsibility for ensuring that it is achieved.

The level of detail in the series of booklets which make up the Critical Skills Programme is impressive. Not only is it well-grounded in theory and research, but it elaborates each of the nine characteristics through detailed lesson plans, suggested 'coaching scripts' for teachers, a process for creating a 'full value contract' to make the classroom 'a safe place to be' and fully elaborated sets of 'Quality Criteria' for adaptation for use in the classroom. Add to this an impressive array of tools and planning formats and it is easy to see why the Critical Skills Programme has made such an impact in some Local Authorities in Scotland.

Principles of the cooperative classroom

Cooperative learning is making something of a comeback in Scottish schools. From a point in the 1960s and 1970s when it was seen as the norm, as primary and secondary education was transformed as a result of the Primary Memorandum (Scottish Education Department, 1965) and comprehensivisation, respectively, through the backlash of the 'New Right' in 1980s and 1990s (Boyd, 2005) when 'direct (interactive) teaching' was promoted by HMI[E] (1996), it has taken Assessment is for Learning and A Curriculum for Excellence to create the conditions for cooperative learning to flourish once again.

In identifying some key principles of cooperative learning, it is worth stating that it is not simply about classroom management or the organisation of tables and chairs. Even in many classrooms where the desks/tables are permanently arranged in groups, there is no guarantee that cooperative learning is taking place. If cooperative learning is about anything, it is about pedagogy, about a philosophy of education which places active pupil engagement and deep learning at the heart of the process. Thus, *the cooperative classroom* will embody the following principles:

- *Cooperative learning promotes cognitive development* This principle is fundamental and is based on the work of Vygotsky. It presupposes that a cooperative classroom will focus on deep rather than surface learning, will promote self- and peer-assessment based on public criteria and will build in opportunities for learners to demonstrate/perform/display their understanding.

- *Dialogue* Dialogue, teacher–pupil and pupil–pupil, is the *raison d'être* of cooperative learning. The skills of discussion need to be made explicit, and the pupils must be supported to acquire these skills. Alexander (2006) uses the phrases *learning-talk* and *teaching-talk* and sees dialogue as part of the repertoire of pupils and teachers. Black and Wiliam (1998) promote dialogue as being a broader and more fundamental element than simply questioning. The role of talk in learning and the provision of structures, frameworks, protocols and scaffolding for pupils to enable them to learn effectively through dialogue is a key principle of cooperative learning.

- *Interdependence and responsibility for one's own and others' learning* The group or the team is more than simply a random collection of learners, united only by the geography of the classroom. Nor is it an organisational device to label or separate learners on the basis of some test score or other putative measure of prior attainment. The Ward–Craigen approach makes an explicit virtue of 'heterogenous groups' because they claim that they 'promote more elaborate thinking and explanations, and provide opportunities for students to develop feelings of mutual concern' (Ward and Craigen, 1999, p. 48). Thus the group works best when all the members take responsibility for the learning of the whole group. Indeed, the Critical Skills Programme would extend this to the whole classroom community.

- *The role of the teacher changes* The teacher's role changes from context to context. In the cooperative classroom, the teacher does not solve problems for pupils. Instead, the teacher is willing to take some risks, to intervene only when it is necessary, to refrain from being the answer-giver, to prompt and explore with pupils and to provide the strategies which students will need to solve these genuine problems. There is an implication that, once the learning has been set in motion, the teacher will have enough trust in the learners to let go the reins and allow the learners to become more self-directed.

POINTS FOR REFLECTION

1 Cooperative learning is derived from the work of Vygotsky. Yet, historically, some secondary school subjects have tended to encourage pupils to work individually, often in silence. Are some subjects simply not suited to cooperative learning? Or are there other reasons for this?

2 Which of the programmes featured in this chapter do you think offers the most interesting approach to cooperative learning? Why?

3 What do you think of the principles of *the cooperative classroom?*

10 The intelligent classroom

> Four-year-olds in the Stanford preschool were brought into a room one by one, a marshmallow was put on the table in front of them, and they were told, 'You can eat it if you want, but if you don't eat it until after I run an errand, you can have two when I return.'
>
> Some fourteen years later, as they were graduating from high school, the children who ate the marshmallow right away were compared with those who waited and got two ... Those children who had waited for the marshmallows, compared to those who hadn't, had scores averaging a remarkable 210 points higher (out of a possible 1600) on the SAT, the college entrance exam.
>
> **Daniel Goleman, *Emotional Intelligence***

Intelligence: an enduring myth?

Of all of the concepts most enduringly linked to schooling, intelligence is perhaps the most enduring. It operates at a number of levels: the common-sense, the psychological, the structural, the political and the cultural. It was T.S. Eliot who wrote in 1948 that 'the function of schooling is to preserve the class and select elite' (*Notes Towards a Definition of Culture*). Issues of selection, elitism and the British class system have never been far away from the concept of intelligence. Indeed, the notion of selection, has long been seen as inseparable from schooling and it was this very imperative, in France in the nineteenth century, along with a scientific movement which sought to measure the Universe and everything within it, which led to the first attempts to devise intelligence tests. It seemed logical that if schools were to select students then there should be objective and scientific tests which might be used to predict the future performance of students in the education system.

Since the Second World War, politically, parties on the Right in British politics have favoured selection. The Conservative Party has always been in favour of Grammar schools, created by selecting pupils at age eleven by means of the 11+ (a mix of standardised and IQ tests), a fact borne out by the furore within the UK party in 2007 when the leader, David Cameron, suggested that the party distance itself from Grammar schools since there was no evidence that they increased social cohesion or promoted social mobility. However, prior to the Second World War, all parties subscribed to what was then seen to be a Truth, namely that children were born with different levels of intelligence, which then interacted with their environment, resulting in an IQ which was fixed, measurable and predictable over time. This was used, naturally, to select pupils (normally at age 12 in Scotland by means of the qualifying exam, the 'Quali') for junior or senior secondary schools. Indeed, it was not until the mid 1960s that the practice of universal measurement of IQs ceased, and with the implementation of comprehensive schools, selection also was abandoned.

At around this time in the 1960s and 1970s, a number of psychologists began to publish challenges to the concept of IQ. Most notable among them was the Harvard academic Howard Gardner, who introduced the concept of Multiple Intelligences (1983). The present author has written about the importance of Multiple Intelligences (Boyd, 2005) and this chapter will address some of the other important theories which have challenged the traditional concept of intelligence.

At around the same time in Israel, Reuven Feuerstein was dismissing the concept of static, objective intelligence tests which served, in his view, to limit the potential of the child, and he devised, building on Vygotsky's concept of the *zone of proximal development*, dynamic tests where the examiner interacted with the person to try to find out what s/he might be capable of with the mediation of a significant other. Feuerstein's tests were called *Learning Assessment Propensity Devices*, based on his theory, supported now by recent research on the human brain, that intelligence is not fixed, that it can grow, it can be altered and that it is 'plastic' (Feuerstein *et al.*, 2002).

More recently, Carol Dweck (1999) and Hart *et al.* (2004) have challenged the concept of intelligence in different ways.

Dweck's *Self-Theories* explores how students' 'implicit theories' of intelligence have a significant impact not only on how they learn but on how they handle failure and setbacks. Hart and colleagues reviewed the literature on intelligence (see Chapter 3) before exploring the ways in which teachers' views of intelligence can impact on their classroom behaviour, expectations and interactions with learners.

The Scottish Network on Able Pupils (SNAP) Newsletter (Issue 23, Spring 2004) was devoted entirely to the issue of implicit theories of intelligence. It drew on the work of Jerome Bruner (1996) and Robert Steinberg (1990), the latter suggesting:

> Implicit theories ... reside in the minds of individuals, whether as definitions or otherwise. Such theories need to be uncovered rather than invented because they already exist, in some form, in people's heads.
>
> (p. 54)

Thus, implicit theories, or common-sense view, Steinberg argues, are there, in our heads. Bruner calls them 'everyday, intuitive theories about how our minds work' (Bruner, 1996, p. 5). At a conference in Glasgow in June 2007, Carol Dweck argued that the concept of 'self-esteem' had become misrepresented and, in particular, looked at the relationship between self-esteem and praise. She argued that, while praise should not be seen as 'the villain of the piece', if it is directed at the wrong target it could have the opposite effect to that intended by the praiser. In fact, it is interesting that SNAP should have chosen to focus on implicit theories of intelligence, since, some three years later, Dweck suggests that the more able learners were most at risk when they had 'an entity (or fixed) theory of intelligence' since when they encountered failure they were more likely to give up, arguing that they were simply 'not good' at the subject/activity. This would be exacerbated if the same learners were used to being praised for 'being clever'. Dweck's suggestion is not only that learners should be encouraged to have an 'incremental' (or growth) theory of intelligence, but that praise should be directed at effort or strategies. Test scores, Dweck argues, do not predict the future; the hard work, drive and determination of the young people predict the future.

Reuven Feuerstein: the dynamic assessment of cognitive modifiability

Reuven Feuerstein *et al.* (2002) have produced the most trenchant and thorough critique of the conventional concept of intelligence and its link to learning. Their challenge to 'conventional psychometric practices' (p. 4) is based on the belief that they 'reflect conceptualizations of intelligence as a generalized and stable phenomenon' (p. 4) and on the 'evidence accumulated over the last several decades that the assumption underlying the psychometric measurement procedure is highly suspect' (p. 5). IQ tests, therefore, in their view are questionable since 'there is little reason to assume or accept that performance on such tests provides a stable or reliable measure of future performance' (p. 7). Feuerstein *et al.* are similarly critical of traditional psychological approaches to the measurement of cognitive functioning. For them, this is a key issue for they see cognition as 'a pre-requisite for adaptation' (p. 8).

The issue of *labelling* is addressed by Feuerstein *et al.* They describe how the label of 'mental retardation' has, historically, been 'the most powerful determining force in the individual's personality and social interactions' (p. 12) and cite Hobbs who suggests that in the American education system:

> ... the label of mental retardation tends to doom children to a life of educational interventions which do not lift them out of that condition, and predict the same for their progeny.
> (Hobbs, quoted in Feuerstein *et al.*, 2002, p.12)

They use a quotation from Goldstein to sum up the enduring nature of such labels: 'the process of labelling is a formal procedure, the removal of labels is not' (p. 12).

Neuroscience – what can it tell us about the brain?

If the 1990s was the 'decade of the brain' (Boyd, 2005), the early part of the twenty-first century has seen a rise in scepticism about the very idea of 'brain-based learning'. In 2002 the Economic and Social Research Council (ESRC) published

Neuroscience and Education: Issues and Opportunities as part of its Teaching and Learning Research Programme. In Scotland, the Scottish Council for Research in Education (SCRE) published *Neuroscience and Education: What can Brain Science Contribute to Learning and Teaching* (Hall, 2005) as part of its 'Spotlight' series. What appears to be happening at the present time is an attempt by some academics (Christie, 2007; Coffield *et al.*, 2004) and policy-influencers (HMIE) to look to neuroscience to provide hard, scientific evidence to discredit approaches to learning, often grouped together under the heading of 'brain-based learning', which have found favour in classrooms. The argument they advance is two-fold; first, the phrase 'brain-based learning' is tautologous since, they claim, there is no other kind of learning; it all takes place in the brain. Secondly, they argue that unless neuroscience, through its use of MRI scans and other technologies for accessing the living brain, can verify claims made by those who propose ideas such as *learning styles, multiple intelligences, integrated movement, mind mapping* and a number of others such as *neurolinguistic programming,* these should be discounted, if not discredited. While on the one hand this may seem little more than a fascinating academic argument, it also has the potential to unsettle teachers. What are they to believe? If they have become exponents of learning styles or mind mapping or even what some people have called *brain gym,* have they to stop because neuroscience cannot verify the effectiveness of these approaches? Both of the claims made on behalf of neuroscience are contestable. Hannaford, a biologist, in her most influential book *Smart Moves: Why learning is Not all in Your Head,* has argued:

> Thinking and learning are not all in our head. On the contrary, the body plays an integral part in all our intellectual processes from our earliest movements *in utero* right through to old age. It is our body's senses that feed the brain environmental information with which to form an understanding of the world and from which to draw when creating new possibilities. And it is our movements that not only express knowledge and facilitate greater cognitive function, they actually grow the brain and they increase in complexity. Our entire brain structure is intimately connected to and grown by the movement mechanisms within our body.
>
> (Hannaford, 2005, pp. 15,16)

Hannaford goes onto develop an approach called *integrated movement,* similar in many ways to *brain gym.* She cites a number of studies supportive of the approach, but none of them from a neuroscientific standpoint. The questions is: is neuroscience the only point of reference?

This takes us to the second contestable issue. The term *neuromyth* has been coined to describe claims about the brain and learning for which there is no scientific evidence. Rightly, it includes misinterpretations of otherwise scientifically reputable notions such as the right and left hemispheres of the brain (see Boyd, 2005), which some people have over simplified to such an extent that they talk of right- and left-brain learning, almost as if there are two separate functioning brains. In fact, the issue is much more complex. MRI scans show that, at any one time, areas in the whole brain are active, but that some functions, particularly those to do with aspects of language development, are located on one side of the brain. What those non-neuroscientists who promote neuroscience often fail to make clear is the conclusion of the ESRC report:

> ... considerable caution needs to be applied when attempting to transfer concepts between neuroscience and education. Such attempts need to be well informed by expertise from both fields.
> (Economic and Social research Council, 2002, p. 15)

The conclusion of Hall (2005) is more cautiously optimistic:

> It seems clear that the sceptics are right to criticise some of the wilder claims made for the place of neuroscience in education ... There are some grounds for optimism: neuroscientific findings are beginning to shed some light on a few particular areas of learning, including language learning, literacy, numeracy and dyslexia, and the link between the emotions and learning.
> (p. 7)

Coffield *et al.* (2004) produced a highly critical report on their review of the literature on 'learning styles', an approach that has come to be associated with the term 'brain-based learning'. The systematic and critical review found that there was little convincing evidence for the claims of most of the learning styles programmes analysed (with the exceptions of the approach developed by Entwistle, a member of the steering group for the project). While critical of most of the learning styles schemes, for their lack of research base, for their profit-inspired overblown claims, for their loose use of terminology or for their conceptual confusion, the report does not advise teachers to abandon the whole notion of learning styles. Instead, using Entwistle as a positive example, teachers should be cautious of applying labels to learners (visual, auditory or kinaesthetic, for example); the report suggests that, as long as teachers use the learning styles concept to enable them to change the learning–teaching environment rather than to categorise learners, this can be beneficial.

This whole issue puts into sharp relief the relationship between research and practice. Are teachers to use only those practices for which there is uncontestable research evidence? If so, is the reverse also true? Should teachers abandon, for example, the practice of 'setting' pupils into classes on the basis of test scores because the research evidence in favour of the efficacy of this practice is almost non-existent? Perhaps the interplay of theory, research and professional practice is more subtle and more complex than this and what is needed is less dismissiveness and more dialogue.

Daniel Goleman: *Emotional Intelligence – improving learning* in Scottish Borders Council

Scottish Borders Council has for some time been at the forefront of developments designed to improve learning and teaching in its schools. Its approach focuses on effective learning and teaching, drawing on the work of Daniel Goleman, Reuven Feuerstein and Howard Gardner, among others. An extensive programme of CPD was put in place by members of the Quality Improvement team, supported by informative leaflets devised by Anne-Theresa Lawrie.

A common dilemma for educators is how much knowledge about the workings of the brain the average teacher needs to have to make the classroom a place where learning is supported. The Scottish Borders Council (SBC) leaflets go into some considerable detail, which will be seen by some to be excessive. But the leaflets' purpose is to be supportive, not directive. Teachers, increasingly, want to know the *why* of new ideas. Why should they take account of emotional intelligence? Why is a certain approach likely to work with, for example, disaffected or unpredictable youngsters? What kinds of interventions on their part seem most likely to be successful, and why?

An edited version of the SBC leaflets may serve to show how one authority has tried to support its CPD programme with some messages from research.

WHAT IS LEARNING?

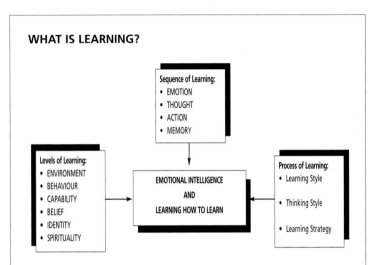

The model above is proposed by M Brearley where Emotional Intelligence and the Process of Learning are merged to promote effective learning for pupils. This model is discussed on pp 2–34 of 'Emotional Intelligence in the Classroom'. The structure of learning according to this model provides the capability to work at the level of belief, which is one major factor in determining our feeling and emotions.

Emotions and Learning
There is a direct relationship between how we structure our lessons and the way the brain works:
- Students need to be ready to learn – relaxed and receptive to the stimulation of their environment
- Stimulation should be multi-sensory – giving students the chance to use their preferred learning style

- Feedback should be immediate, specific and reinforce learning
- Learning should be continually reviewed and concerned with how the learning is taking place, the learning strategy and the success of learning
- Learning should be mediated through 'how' questions
- Each lesson should contain several starts and finishes
- Provide choice – not in 'what' is learnt but in 'how' it is learnt.

The structure of our lesson will create the thinking that leads to learning. How we think, our preferred style, is a consequence of the brain being able to think in different ways. These are Serial Thinking (IQ), Associative Thinking (EQ) and Unitive Thinking (co-operation between EQ and IQ). Serial Thinking, Associative Thinking and Unitive Thinking are discussed in detail on pp 36–42 of 'Emotional Intelligence in the Classroom'. The importance of emotional memory is also discussed on pp 38–41 of this book and contains pupil activities for enhancing memory.

The following diagram illustrates how emotions affect performance:

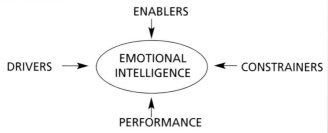

ENABLERS these are emotions such as self-awareness, optimism, relaxation and self-esteem

DRIVERS these are emotions such as motivation, ambition, foresight and determination

CONSTRAINERS these are emotions such as pessimism, anxiety, fear and low self-esteem

Principles of the intelligent classroom

The intelligent classroom is one in which the concept of intelligence is not hidden or assumed. No pupils are judged on the basis of an outdated understanding of intelligence, and 'common-sense' notions have no place. Euphemisms that have traditionally surrounded the application of labels to pupils – such as 'bright' or 'dull' or 'brainy' or 'thick' or 'backward' or 'high flyer' – are avoided. Knowledge of the learning process is shared with the learner, and the concept of metacognition is discussed. Factors which can affect the success of learning are also shared, the affective and the cognitive domains, self-theories and goal setting, independence and interdependence. The classroom is a place where intelligent decisions are made, based on knowledge rather than myth and where optimism about the capacity of all pupils to learn is pervasive:

- *Self-theories* Pupils should be introduced to the old and the new conceptions of intelligence. They should be aware that intelligence is not fixed and that they can influence their own cognitive development. They should be confident when they encounter a difficulty in learning that giving up or blaming some third party or external circumstance is unlikely to help. Instead, they should be able to analyse the 'failure', re-group (perhaps with the help of others) and try a new strategy.
- *Multiple intelligences* The concept of multiple intelligences is well-established if not universally accepted. For the teacher, the academic arguments are around whether the eight (or so) intelligences identified by Howard Gardner are, in fact, intelligences. The main benefit to teachers is to help them to see each child as unique, each with a different profile of strengths and weaknesses, and each with a capacity to be a successful learner. The intelligences are best seen as 'entry points' into the learning process. If the *linguistic* and *logical/mathematical* intelligences, traditionally dominant in formal schooling, do not enable a pupil to understand something, then approaching it through one of the other intelligences may do so. It is this interpretation of *multiple intelligences* which has caused some people to see them as being linked to learning styles.

- *Learning is not all in the brain* The emotions, music, dance, physical activity and, as Hannaford (2002) would say, the 'brain/heart interface' are all important in learning – although it must be acknowledged that this view is contested. What is certainly true is that there is a clear relationship between the 'affective' and the 'cognitive' domains. Some psychologists will argue that one takes precedence over the other. Few educationists will argue that the emotions are not part of learning. When we as teachers try to create a climate for learning or an ethos of achievement in our classrooms, we are acknowledging this link.

POINTS FOR REFLECTION

1 Is intelligence the 'final frontier'? Do we need to challenge the myths in the same way we did on race, gender, disability? Do commonsense notions get in the way of understanding?

2 What do you see as being Dweck's contribution to the debate? Should students/pupils explore the concept of intelligence as part of their learning?

3 Is 'emotional intelligence' a helpful concept? What insights does it offer?

4 What do you think of the principles of *the intelligence classroom?*

11 The global classroom

> 'Going on an Expotition?' said Pooh eagerly.
> 'I don't think I've ever been on one of those.
> Where are we going to on this Expotition?'
> 'Expedition, silly old Bear. It's got an 'x' in it.'
> 'Oh!' said Pooh. 'I know.' But he didn't really.
> 'We're going to discover the North Pole.'
> 'Oh!' said Pooh again. 'What is the North Pole?'
> he asked.
> 'It's just a thing you discover,' said Christopher
> Robin carelessly, not being quite sure himself.
>
> Benjamin Hoff, *The Te of Piglet*

The big issues

Of all the classrooms, *the global classroom* may well seem, for most teachers, the most expendable. After all, it doesn't easily fit with the existing subject areas of A Curriculum for Excellence. The previous national curriculum programme, 5–14, had an area called Environmental Studies, which, on the face of it, should have incorporated the global dimension, and, indeed, this is where most environmental projects were located. But, the global dimension is much more than the occasional environmental studies topic. It is, in many respects, the core of all learning, encompassing what it is to be human and to live, interdependently, with all other humans on the planet. The phrase *global citizen* may in some instances be used rather glibly, but it contains concepts and dispositions which may be crucial to the continuing progress of the human race.

Let us look at some of the elements of the global dimension. In the early part of the twenty-first century, there are few more important issues emerging world-wide than climate change and global warming. While there is something uplifting about working to 'save the planet', attracting the enthusiastic support of former vice-Presidents like Al Gore and pop stars like Madonna, the other major challenges have less hope attached to them. Poverty in the developing world, and conflict, particularly between Islamic fundamentalists and Western nations, involving invasions, war, terrorism, suicide bombings and hostage taking, all seem altogether more intractable problems to solve. And yet, education is taking on many of these issues. From the *eco-schools* initiative to *The Global Dimension*, from *citizenship* to *fair trade*, pupils in Scottish schools are engaged with big issues.

In the late 1990s, the Institute for Global Ethics in Camden, Maine, conducted an international survey across 80 countries. People were asked to list what they viewed as the key issues for the new century. Regardless of wealth, country or religion, people identified broadly the same concerns. The top six were these:

- mass destruction
- environmental sustainability
- population growth
- north–south divide
- education reform
- breakdown in public and private morality.

The consensus around these issues was remarkable and is further evidence, if it were needed, that global issues have become central to people's concerns, world-wide.

But what are teachers expected to do in the classroom? What advice is there available? In 2007, Learning and Teaching Scotland (LTS) published a pack entitled *The Global Dimension in the Curriculum*. It consisted of a paper subtitled 'Educating the global citizen, a practitioner resource and working towards an open, participatory ethos: case studies'. 'Educating the global citizen' provided a rationale for *The Global Dimension*'s inclusion in the curriculum. The document made the point early on that 'the global dimension is not an additional subject … it should be developed across the curriculum' (p. 1). Immediately, the challenge therefore is for secondary schools, with their fixation on subjects (Boyd, 2005); primary schools have always been more receptive to the notion of 'cross-cutting themes'. Education for the global dimension, claims the document:

is an active process which encourages young people to:

- develop knowledge and understanding of the interdependence of our own and other societies, including the effects of global inequality, poverty and conflict;
- develop and practise skills and capabilities that enable investigation of issues, problem-solving and working co-operatively with others in appropriate contexts;
- gain experience of, develop and adopt values and dispositions that are crucial to a just and democratic society in a sustainable world;
- take thoughtful and responsible action which aims to contribute to the achievement of a just and caring world, and the development of friendship between peoples.

(p. 1)

This series of bullet points is worthy of some careful analysis. The first issue which arises is the politically sensitive nature of the topics to be covered. It is hard to see how 'inequality, poverty and conflict' could be addressed in a classroom setting without consideration of values, both the pupils' and those of different cultures and nations. The expectation of the teacher is high. S/he would have to be able to create a climate in the classroom where it would be possible for pupils with quite different views to be able to express them openly without fear of ridicule or attack. A recent study carried out by a doctoral student from the Institute of Education, University of London, reported in the *Guardian* (Shepherd, 'What does Britain expect?', Tuesday 17.07.07) showed that views among pupils on the issue of citizenship and patriotism highlight the uncertainty teachers feel about raising such controversial issues in the classroom. The chief executive of the Citizenship Foundation suggests that 'we are not giving teachers professional preparation to deal with these issues. It takes real confidence to lead students in discussions on pieces of writing about these very complex issues. You can't just rush it through with the register.'

Clearly, the suggestion of the LTS document, that young people should 'develop and practise skills and capabilities', makes certain assumptions about pedagogy. 'Working co-operatively with others' clearly signals an expectation that young people will be able to interact with one another 'in appropriate contexts', which might include anything from debates, mock trials, UN assemblies, role-play, as well as small-group discussion.

The notion that these same young people should 'develop and adopt values and dispositions ... crucial to a just and democratic society' begs all sorts of important questions. Which values? Whose values? Are all democratic societies just (and vice-versa)? Are democracies more or less likely to work towards a sustainable world? It is not difficult to see how complex this whole area is for teachers, and for young people.

Finally, there is, in the final bullet point, a call to action. The idea that the young people should be proactive is an interesting one. In Scotland, there have been examples of young people taking a campaigning role in oppositions to dawn raids on homes of asylum seekers and many small projects in support of fair trade. *The Global Dimension* seems to be suggesting that 'thoughtful and responsible action' should be among the outcomes of this approach.

The spiral curriculum

The LTS document outlines eight 'key concepts which should form the basis of a spiral curriculum' (p. 1). There are clear links, conceptually, to the work of Jerome Bruner here. Bruner's work came to prominence in the 1960s when the United States, stung by the Russian launch of the Sputnik in 1957, ordered a root-and-branch review of teaching methods in American schools. The idea that the Russians had out-thought American scientists and won the 'space race' prompted the National Academy of Science to hold a conference in 1959 to discuss how education could contribute to advances in scientific exploration. The chair of the conference was Jerome Bruner, a psychologist at Harvard. The resulting report of the proceedings, *The Process of Education* (Bruner, 1960) was far-reaching in its impact.

Bruner addressed the issue of how science education could become more 'meaningful' (Philips and Soltis, 2004, p. 72). He argued that students should be equipped to tackle the problems of the future and that this would be facilitated if they were able to grasp the *structure* of the discipline. Philips and Soltis (2004) quote the following passage to illustrate Bruner's philosophy:

> Grasping the structure of a subject is understanding it in a way that permits many other things to be related to it immediately. To learn structure, in short, is to learn how things are related ... In

order for a person to be able to recognise the applicability or the inapplicability of an idea to a new situation and to broaden learning thereby, he must have clearly in mind the general nature of the phenomenon with which he is dealing.

(p. 73)

Thus the philosophy of science, argued Bruner, was as important as the outcomes of scientific enquiry.

For Bruner, learning is an active process, with the learner constructing new meanings, building on prior knowledge. This process of building led him to conceive of the curriculum as a *spiral,* with students revisiting ideas and deepening their understanding, making connections, broadening and deepening learning and becoming more aware of the structure of the disciplines within which the learning is taking place.

Key concepts of the global dimension

The LTS document (2007, p. 1) outlines eight key concepts:

- global citizenship
- interdependence
- conflict resolution
- social justice
- diversity
- sustainable development
- human rights
- values and world views.

The opening paragraph of section 1 of the document, 'The purposes of the global dimension in the curriculum', begins with another echo of Bruner:

It is important to help learners to see the connections between the various aspects of their learning, and to encourage them to understand that our actions affect our own physical, social and economic environments and those of other people across the world.

(p. 3)

In a helpful diagram, the document presents the eight key concepts within a framework which attempts to link the global dimension to *A Curriculum for Excellence*'s four key purposes:

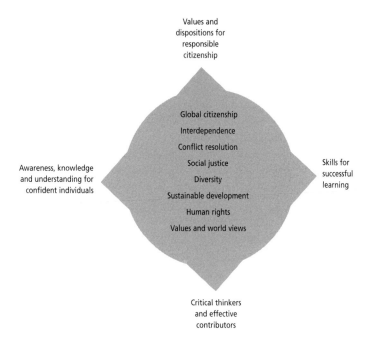

The report's *raison d'être* is a belief that through the global dimension 'links can be made between local and global issues, and it also means that global matters inform what is taught' (p. 3). The document argues that a global perspective can be taken at all stages of learning, from early years to late secondary school and beyond, and suggests that it has implications for pedagogy, with an emphasis on 'more open-ended and active approaches' (p. 6). This is consistent with many of the other perspectives explored in this book, but how exactly can the global dimension fit into the curriculum?

A practitioner resource

The companion document to *Educating the Global Citizen* is an interesting one. Its scope is far wider than the title suggests; it is not simply a *how to* manual but rather addresses some key issues for schools to consider. A glance at its table of contents in outline illustrates the scope of the LTS report:

• The aims of the global dimension in the curriculum
• Recognising and developing existing good practice
• Development of a whole school ethos
• Learning and teaching approaches
• Managing the global dimension
• Recognising and evaluating existing work.

However, it is the detail which is impressive in this unassuming report. The section on 'Development of a whole school ethos' suggests that 'an open, participatory ethos' is necessary, and argues that 'Leadership in the global dimension can come from individuals throughout the school community' (p. 7). It also argues for a 'commitment to values', pointing out that 'Some schools have successfully involved children and young people in developing the school's value statement' (p. 7). Interestingly, the document addresses an issue which always comes up in discussions with teachers, namely how to respond to world events. In recent years, the attack on the twin towers of the World Trade Centre in New York on what has become known as 9/11; the tsunami in the Far East on Boxing Day 2004; and more recent floods, earthquakes and storms, in areas from New Orleans to southern England, have all made an impact on the consciousness of people around the world. Teachers often ask 'How can we respond to such events? Can we deviate from our forward plans or from our exam syllabus and focus the pupils' learning on these topical events?' This report is suggesting that such events may provide excellent opportunities for pupils to engage in 'active global citizenship' and gives websites of NGOs (non-governmental organisations) and other organisations which help with resources for schools. In other words, if the global dimension is seen not simply as being about content but also about pedagogy, then teachers will have the confidence to access resources and adjust their plans to focus the pupils' learning on real events.

The section on 'Teaching and learning approaches' is one of the most helpful in the whole document. In this section, a range of 'participatory learning' approaches is considered:

- Teaching controversial issues
- Philosophy for children
- Media literacy
- Role-plays, games and simulations
- Partnerships in school linking
- Cooperative learning
- Critical skills programme

(p. 11)

Each of these is reviewed, the principles are presented and resources/additional reading lists are supplied.

The final section, 'Recognising and evaluating existing work', is perhaps the most extensive. For each of the sub-sections listed below, there are sub-sub-sections which typically include:

- Whole-school setting
- Classroom setting
- Children and young people.

Not all the sub-sections lend themselves to this framework (e.g. 'Questions for professional reflection') but most do:

- Environment and community
- Pastoral care and inclusion
- Democracy and decision-making
- Curricular
- Whole school and extra-curricular
- Procurement, resource management and social justice
- Staff support
- Quality assurance.

Thus, for example, the section on procurement, etc. challenges the school to look at its purchase of materials and resources; the teacher to consider how resources within the classroom are used (and re-used?); and children to consider how they deal with, for example, food, drink and litter while at school.

Global warming: a 'no-brainer' or a contested issue?

In Chapter 6 we looked at the teaching of a controversial issue, namely the Holocaust. Henry Maitles has argued that teachers should not shy away from controversial issues, and it is through such experiences that they can begin to form and articulate their values and moral positions. In recent years, the terrorist attacks in New York, Bali, London, Madrid, the ongoing conflicts in Afghanistan and Iraq, the assassination of Benazir Bhutto and the almost daily atrocities in various parts of the world where internal differences remain unsolved – all present opportunities for teachers in classrooms to explore the implications with their pupils. When events such as Live Aid take place or when the annual Comic Relief extravaganza fills our television screens with images of poverty, disadvantage and deprivation, the controversies surrounding aid, the gap between the developed and the developing world, and the responsibilities of world leaders to act in a long-term way to promote greater equality, are brought to the forefront. But many would suggest that climate change is no longer a contested issue. Surely, now that the US has finally, it would appear, signed up to the Kyoto Protocol following the summit in Bali in November 2007, everyone must agree that climate change is the number one global issue?

Not so. The DVD made by former US vice-President Al Gore has been distributed free to all schools in Great Britain. But not everyone is grateful for this high-quality, and very well made, film. Some have suggested that it is propaganda and that some of its claims are debatable. Others have suggested that Gore's motives may be less than altruistic given the absence of a track record on the issue while he was in office. A controversial contribution to the issue took place at the Royal Society Christmas Lecture at Edinburgh University in December 2007. *The Times Educational Supplement Scotland* (Smith, 2007) reported the lecture under the headline 'Johnny causes storm in lecture on climate change' and described how Johnny Ball, a TV presenter, well-known for his popularisation of science over the years, took the opportunity during his lecture to children to attack 'greens ... who want society to collapse'. He argued that CO_2 was being 'demonised' and questioned whether there was enough of it in the atmosphere to have a damaging effect. He challenged the accepted wisdom that the polar ice caps were melting, arguing that the earth had barely heated up 0.5 degrees in the last five years and bemoaned the fact that 'environmentalism' was taking over in schools.

The reaction of the academics from Edinburgh University was interesting. Some condemned Ball out of hand, suggesting his presentation was 'a rant in denial of climate change' and that his opinions would put 'fear, uncertainty and doubt in the minds of young children'. Professor Mary Bownes, on the other hand, suggested that his comments would 'stimulate debate', a view echoed by one of the pupils who said it was good to be 'challenged'.

The issue here is not who is right, Al Gore or Johnny Ball, neither of whom would be termed an 'expert' on climate change. The issue is surely one of evidence and the balance of probability. As teachers, we have a duty to develop young people's critical thinking, to enable them to weigh up evidence from different sources, to give them the skills of analysis and synthesis and to help them make informed choices. To that extent, we might say Johnny Ball's intervention was useful; but the fact that he did not produce evidence for his own assertions renders his criticism of the greens invalid and makes his intervention, especially to a young audience, suspect. A teacher wishing to look at global warming as an issue would certainly benefit from having access to both Al Gore's DVD and Johnny Ball's lecture.

80:20 Development in an Unequal World – A resource for teachers

A real, practical problem for teachers who might wish to create *the global classroom* is finding resources which are suitable for young people and which are copyright-free. While television may provide a regular source of high-quality documentaries on a range of related topics, not all of them are aimed at a younger audience and not all of them are able to be freely copied, even for educational use. The publication *80:20 Development in an Unequal World,* now in its fifth edition, is published in Ireland by the government-funded organisation 80:20 Educating and Acting for a Better World. At 318 pages long, this A4 size publication, edited by Colm Regan, contains an incredible amount of information on a huge range of topics. Its contents pages (beautifully illustrated) give an indication of the scope of the book:

1 Development: the basics
2 Debating development
3 Human rights
4 Sustainable development
5 Politics and development
6 Aid and development
7 Development education
8 The action agenda
9 Trade and development
10 Gender
11 Health
12 Education
13 Arms
14 Millennium development goals
15 Corruptions
16 Identity
17 HIV/Aids
18 Hunger
19 Wealth and poverty
20 Population

There is an accompanying CD containing activities for use in the classroom, including 'stimulus sheets' introducing and exploring key topics.

Pedagogy

The introduction to the book, 'Some ideas for using this book', contains some helpful advice to teachers about *process* as well as *content*. Reference is made to Paulo Freire and Myles Horton, both of whom have argued that education is a 'two-way process, where the ideas and experiences of the learner are an integral and essential element alongside those (of) the teacher' (Regan, 2006, p. 8). The introduction goes on to say that 'the most important thing that can be done ... is to ask critical questions' (p. 8).

Each section in the book begins with *stimulus pages* which might contain:

- cartoons
- statistical summaries
- summary debate pages
- 'big ideas'
- ten facts
- keynote debates.

These pages are photocopiable and contain the kind of information which it would take a teacher hours to pull together from a range of sources. What is also helpful is the suggested teaching approaches, including small-group discussion, whole-class debates, comparing-and-contrasting two different photographs, creation of wall displays which are presented to the rest of the class, examining case studies of real people and real events, etc. There is nothing prescriptive in the book; its aim is to present data. Indeed, the short section (p. 27) headed 'Caution with data', is one of the most helpful in the whole book. It warns the reader (teachers or community workers) that no presentation of data is wholly neutral. The very decision as to how the data are to be presented, the units of measurement used, for example, contain value judgements: 'statistics never speak for themselves' (p. 27).

One of the most controversial issues addressed in the book is HIV/Aids. Many teachers would find this a more controversial issue than, for example, poverty or arms. The section on HIV/Aids is one of the longest and most detailed in the book. It takes Zambia as its main focus and presents two case studies of women with Aids. Statistics on the prevalence of Aids in Zambia are followed by a discussion of the factors which contribute to the spread of Aids in that country, including:

- high levels of poverty
- the high mobility of specific social groups
- socio-cultural beliefs and practices
- stigma
- information, education and communication
- gender issues
- prison.

The world statistics on HIV/Aids are presented, followed by a breakdown of the prevalence of the disease within Africa as a whole, the link between poverty and HIV/Aids and some facts on *transmission*. The rest of the chapter is a detailed account of Zambia's experience, the impact of HIV/Aids, the response of the Government and, finally, some more case studies.

As a whole, the book represents an invaluable resource for teachers; more importantly, it offers a perspective on the world and on the role of education which transcends the traditional academic curriculum. It is not about knowledge for its own sake (learning to know) but about how we apply our learning in the interests of the planet (learning to do). Above all, it demands that we look at the interdependence of human beings (learning to live together) and challenges each and every one of us to look at ourselves to find our common humanity (learning to be).

Principles of the global classroom

The global classroom is one in which the process is as important as the content. While, undoubtedly, the issues which are covered in *The Global Dimension* and in *80:20 Development in an Unequal World* are, in a very real sense, life-and-death; it is how the pupils deal with the evidence, how they evaluate sources of information, how they form judgements and how they develop their value positions (and accommodate others') which will determine how they choose to deal with decisions they will make now and in the future. For these reasons, pedagogy is critical in the global classroom:

- *A community of enquiry* The work of Matthew Lipman (1982) is predicated on the assumption, first articulated by Jerome Bruner, that young children are capable of dealing with abstract concepts if these are presented in ways and in contexts that make them accessible. The global classroom is a safe environment in which controversial issues can be addressed within a culture of respect. The role of the teacher is key; didactic teaching has little place in the global classroom. Instead, the teacher will facilitate learning through discussion, role-play, debates, mock UN general assemblies, and will provide resources from a range of places, which young people can learn to interrogate and to evaluate. The availability of different media and new technology, notably the internet, has opened up a range of resources to teachers.

But the internet brings with it new challenges, not least in the evaluation of sources of information. Cooperative learning, discussion, listening and challenging one another's views will be the staple of the global classroom.

- *Links with the outside world* The global classroom is in a real sense a classroom without walls. Linking with other countries in the developing world is one of the most common ways of introducing the global dimension. The Learning and Teaching Scotland publication suggests that school linking projects are a good thing but reminds us that they need to be carefully considered, sensitive to the needs of the partner school and formed on the basis of equality of decision-making. They should provide opportunities for two-way learning and be less concerned with fund-raising than on sustainable, mutual support. (**www.britishcouncil.org/globalschools-about.htm**)

- *Commitment to values* While a strong feature of Scottish education continues to be a commitment to values, often referred to as *ethos,* this is often seen as a whole-school issue. There is no doubt that the global classroom will be more likely to flourish in a supportive whole-school ethos; but the ethos of the classroom is, arguably, even more important. The role of the teacher in creating a culture where views are respected, where opinions (but not the person) can be challenged, where evidence is valued and where ideas are considered in their complexity with no rush towards simplistic conclusion, is central to the creation of the global classroom. Many teachers are comfortable in this role; others, perhaps because of demands to produce 'results' or because of lack of confidence in their abilities to work in such a fluid situation, may wish to undertake CPD activities, or work cooperatively with colleagues. Many teachers, and others, working in early years and primary environments are, because of their training, more comfortable in this role than some of their secondary colleagues. It seems to be an obvious opportunity for cross-sectoral cooperation.

POINTS FOR REFLECTION

1 For many young people, global issues are at the top of their agenda. How can we, as teachers, reflect this in the classroom...and, at the same time, make learning more *relevant*?

2 If we were to address more global issues in the classroom, what would be the implications for pedagogy?

3 What do you think of the principles of *the global classroom?*

Conclusion

> 'Clever!' said Eyore scornfully, putting a foot heavily on his three sticks. 'Education!' said Eyore bitterly, jumping on his sticks. 'What is Learning?' asked Eyore, as he kicked his twelve sticks into the air. 'A thing Rabbit knows! Ha!'
> **A. A. Milne, *Winnie the Pooh***

The challenge of the final chapter

This may be the final chapter of the book but it is unlikely that it will contain the last word on *the learning classroom*. While it has been suggested that classrooms have changed only slightly, and very slowly, over the past century or more, it is likely that new technologies will hasten the pace of change in the twenty-first century. New terms such as *e-learning, e-portfolios* and even *e-pedagogy* have emerged to try to accommodate the impact of computers, the world-wide web and other technologies on the classroom. But the classroom remains the main arena in which learning occurs, at least the kinds of learning which are currently valued by society. Eyore's question, 'What is Learning?' remains as pertinent today as it was when A.A. Milne wrote his Pooh stories.

The previous chapters are a clear indication of the range and diversity of expectations placed on teachers. The ten kinds of classrooms explored in this book could quite easily have been augmented by:

- the mind mapping classroom
- the musical classroom
- the creative classroom
- the inclusive classroom
- the health-promoting classroom
- the active classroom
- the confident classroom.

And even this list is unlikely to be exhaustive. But, the longer the list becomes, the less likely any single teacher is to be able to deliver on all of these expectations. One can envisage a classroom teacher, probably a primary school teacher since she is expected to be able to be expert in *all* of the curricular initiatives which Governments devise, waking up, bolt upright in the early hours of a Thursday morning, saying, 'Oh no, it's Thursday, and I haven't done any Enterprise!' It is almost as if each of the ten chapters which have made up the body of this book are envisaged by their 'champions' as the most important of all, and that each of the initiatives has to be 'delivered' separately. Even if there were, at any one time, only ten national and/or local initiatives, they do not take account of the core business of the curriculum, namely the subject/areas, individually or in 'cross-cutting themes'; so where is the time to come from in an already overcrowded curriculum to enable teachers to help pupils to develop as effective, independent learners?

For the last twenty to thirty years in Scotland (and elsewhere across the world), Governments have specified not just the subject areas but the amount of time to be allocated to each. This is often expressed in percentages of the total time (Boyd, 2005), and is often applied on a weekly basis, so that a number of minutes, precisely, is specified. Thus if Her Majesty's Inspectorate of Education were to visit a school and find that in the week(s) they were there one or more subject areas failed to receive its full allocation, critical comment would be made. In the secondary school, this can lead to distortions of time slots (or 'periods') so that they may begin at 10.01 a.m. or 11.53 or 2.32 ... So any expectation to deliver on cross-cutting issues such as those explored in chapters 2 to 11 must be in addition, or complementary, to these subjects, unless the curriculum is conceptualised differently.

The challenge of this chapter is to identify the *principles* which underpin each of the 'classrooms', subject them to critical examination, identify similarities, overlaps and differences and attempt to develop a model of the learning classroom. Put simply, what would an effective teacher do on an ongoing, day-to-day, week-to-week, month-to-month basis to promote effective learning for all of her pupils? What kinds of contexts would provide the best opportunities for the most effective learning? What kind of climate in the school as a whole would support such classrooms and what kind of collegiate professional practices would ensure that, in every school, the whole was more than the sum of its parts?

Howard Gardner has defined synthesis as to 'knit together information from disparate sources into a coherent whole' (2006, p. 46) and he has also argued that 'the mind most at a premium in the twenty-first century will be the mind that can synthesise well' (p. 46). The learning classroom will be a product of many sources of advice, theoretical, research-led and professional. It may be little more than a Utopian dream – the classroom in which everyone is learning, and engaged, pleasurably, in the experience. But teachers create this classroom every day, if only for shorter spells than they would wish. So, will this advice drawn from the most influential thinkers and from actual classrooms, help teachers to create *the learning classroom* everyday?

Ten principles of the learning classroom

Reflective professionals: thinking children

The aim of this book has been to look at the current expectations placed upon teachers in Scottish schools in the form of initiatives designed to improve learning and teaching in the classroom. Each of these expectations are well-meaning, but taken together there is a danger that their impact may not be benign. Whether the initiative is Government-sponsored or is the priority of one Local Authority, whether the source of the advice is Scottish or from somewhere across the world, the teacher in the classroom may experience the same sense of helplessness in the face of initiative overload. So far we have looked at ten possible classrooms which this teacher might be expected to create and we have looked also at some of the principles underpinning each classroom. There are, quite clearly, similarities, overlaps and common elements.

So far I have tried to show how *cognitive development* can be promoted within the classroom environment. Cooperation, social interaction, dialogue and metacognition are at the heart of cognitive development. All children can be successful learners, and knowing about how intelligence really works can help pupils become more resilient in their learning.

In addition, the *affective domain* is crucially important. How pupils see themselves, how they feel about their learning, the classroom climate, the relationships within the classroom, the confidence they have in themselves and their motivation to learn when the going gets tough, are all factors which will be important to the learning classroom.

Finally, the role of the teacher in mediating the learning is central to this whole endeavour. The 'teacher' in this case may be the person, fully qualified, well-versed in theory and practice, with a range of pedagogies on which to draw, and with knowledge and expertise. There may be others involved in helping the child to learn – a parent or carer, a support assistant, a classroom helper, a person from the community. Or it may be another pupil, from the same class or someone older, or younger, who has something to contribute to the learning process. Mediation is a key concept, helping pupils to be able to achieve something that they would not be able to do by themselves.

A Curriculum for Excellence is predicated on the assumption that teachers are reflective professionals who can be trusted to read, reflect, discuss and share their expertise with others, all in the quest to be better at what they do. This series of books was conceived to be part of that process of recognising the capacity of teachers to deal with the *why* as well as the *what* of teaching. Therefore, what follows is not a series of 'tips for teachers' or 'ten handy hints'; instead it is a set of principles drawn from experience, reading, theory and research which might help create *the learning classroom*.

Ten principles of the learning classroom:

1 Relationships based on interdependence and trust
2 Assessment as part of learning
3 Making thinking explicit to promote understanding and deep learning
4 Engagement of learners by challenging and supporting their learning
5 Participation through active learning
6 Learners taking responsibility for their own learning
7 No labels: every child can be a powerful learner
8 Dialogue promoted through collaborative learning
9 Intelligence de-mystified and 'growth' mindsets encouraged
10 Making connections: locally (across subjects) and globally (across continents)

1 Relationships

Relationships are key to a well-managed classroom: mutual respect, unconditional positive regard and a refusal to label individuals, by gender, background, 'intelligence' or, indeed, by any criteria. In the words of pupils, a good teacher 'has faith in you' and 'makes you feel clever' (MacBeath *et al.*, 1997). A classroom built on respect will be a positive, constructive place to learn. Teachers will have a clearer understanding of the causes of underachievement, and pupils will be given the strategies and the dispositions to enable them to be successful learners. Better learning leads to better behaviour.

2 Assessment

Assessment *for* learning, assessment *of* learning and assessment *as* learning have been the focus of what may be one of the most successful pedagogical initiatives ever undertaken nationally in Scotland. Based on the work of Black and Wiliam (1998), it has taken the form of high-quality CPD which appears to have struck a chord with teachers in all sectors. The simple framework of sharing learning goals, feedback, questioning and peer- and self-assessment has had an impact on classrooms. The learning classroom, therefore, is one where the reflective teachers are able to develop a clear rationale for formative assessment and to share it with the learners. Assessment is part of learning, looking forward to help pupils in their next tasks; it is not a verdict or a judgement on what has happened in the past.

3 Thinking

Perhaps the most important principle to emerge from Assessment is for Learning and from the thinking skills literature is that teachers should bring thinking into the open as a way of helping pupils to become autonomous learners. Using the language of thinking, displaying the conduct of a thinker, making time for pupil thinking, using questioning to promote thinking, have all been advocated by one or more proponents of thinking skills. Teachers should model the conduct of a thinker, not pretend to know all the answers. Saying 'That's a good question. I don't know the answer to that. How could we find the answer to that?' may the best way of establishing the principle that being thoughtful is to be valued. As David Perkins (1995) says, we should 'value the conduct of a thinker'.

4 Engagement

Generative topics, 'rich tasks' and challenging contexts are important in engaging learners and engendering commitment to aim for the highest standards. This may involve teachers in looking differently at the content of the learning, working in teams with colleagues from across subjects and across sectors, and presenting challenges to pupils which are engaging and which extend and embed their understanding of key concepts and processes. Alan McLean's observations on motivation are extremely helpful here. If Csikszentmihalyi (1991) is right when he describes *flow* as the coming together of challenge and ability in the correct measures, then teachers should try to engage the pupils not by underestimating what they can do based on past experience, but by having the highest possible expectations of all pupils and the appropriate support either from teachers or pupils.

5 Participation

One of the principles underpinning *A Curriculum for Excellence* is *depth*. A common complaint about the current curriculum is that 'coverage' is all and that pupils are expected to take in too much content. The pressure of exams and testing, real or imagined, encourages a surface approach to learning and often sees pupil understanding as a luxury (becoming ever more dispensable as the exams approach). *A Curriculum for Excellence* has signalled that 'de-cluttering' of the curriculum needs to take place if teachers are to focus on pupil understanding and if pupils are to be given time and opportunities to perform their understanding as their learning progresses. Understanding, or deep learning, is what will equip pupils in the world of the twenty-first century.

6 Pupil responsibility

Peer- and self-assessment, small-group and team learning, think-pair-share and the whole panoply of strategies for cooperative learning are important if the goal is promoting greater pupil autonomy in the learning process. Teachers can facilitate, promote and encourage understanding, but they cannot do it for the learners. Discussion, dialogue and reflection are all key elements of independent learning. Learner autonomy is a goal, and the teacher-as-mediator can lead the learner towards self-reliance. Interdependence and working with others can also help to promote independence. 'What the child can do in collaboration with others today, he can do by himself tomorrow' (Vygotsky, 1962).

7 No labels

The concept of *cognitive challenge* lies at the heart of Cognitive Acceleration through Science Education (CASE), Cognitive Acceleration through Mathematics Education (CAME) and other thinking skills programmes. However, Hart *et al.* (2004) have introduced the concept of *learning without limits,* where teachers try to use pedagogies which do not rely on prior categorisation or labelling of pupils by ability. The aim is to use the range of experiences that all pupils have and to group learners by criteria other than some measure of prior attainment. Essentially, this approach is an assault on the practice of *setting* pupils by 'ability' or 'prior attainment'. Hart *et al.*, like Feuerstein and others, are unconvinced of the merits of sorting pupils out into classes by some arbitrary measure of 'ability'. They are of the view that heterogeneous classes are the best ways to organise learning. They are convinced by watching their *teachers-without-limits* that a mix of experiences and prior attainment is the most fertile mix for learning.

8 Dialogue and collaborative learning

The work of Vygotsky underpins many of the theories of subsequent thinking skills proponents. The notion of learning as a social process where learners construct and re-construct meaning through dialogue, questioning, collaborative working, teamwork, debate and argument is a powerful one. For the teacher it means not only setting up opportunities for such activities to take place but also enabling the learners to acquire the skills to participate fully and actively in such dialogue. Approaches such as *dialogic teaching, cooperative learning* and *critical skills* are all manifestations of the desire to capitalise on the principles of collaborative learning. Thus, when Jerome Bruner advised the American legislature in the early sixties that if they wanted to overtake the USSR in the space race they should educate young people to be critical and creative thinkers, he set in train a process of school education which has allowed younger colleagues such as Howard Gardner and David Perkins to develop their influential theories of Multiple Intelligences and Teaching for Understanding, respectively.

9 Intelligence

Traditionally, the concept of 'intelligence' is rarely discussed in classrooms. There is a kind of 'common-sense', unwritten understanding that everyone knows what it is and that, somehow, some people have more of it than others. What is worse, some of the classes teachers teach will have been organised according to *proxy* measures of intelligence, such as test scores, curricular levels or exam results. So it is hardly surprising that pupils have fixed mindsets, seeing intelligence as fixed, unalterable, predictive of their future achievement and outwith their control. Thus, when they encounter difficulty, they are more likely to blame external factors and give up, too easily. We need to enable them to challenge this mindset.

10 Make connections

Schools can sometimes seem very detached from the 'real world': in their communities but not part of their communities. And the curriculum subject/areas often seem to bear little relation to real life, or, indeed, to one another (in the 1990s, a Local Authority reviewed its curricular materials at Standard Grade and Higher to look for racial or gender stereotypes in text, photographs or illustrations. Physics received a clean bill of health at Standard Grade; there were no human beings at all in the course materials!). Making connections between the curriculum and the lives of pupils, between our community and society and that of other parts of the world, across subjects, and between the way we learn and how subjects work – all of these are necessary to ensure that in *the learning classroom* pupils see the big picture.

Joining up the learning

Inter-disciplinary learning

A feature of classrooms in recent years has been the atomisation of the curriculum, the division into boxes of learning, with so many minutes allocated to each box. Inter-disciplinary learning has been edged out, or relegated to the courses followed by pupils labelled 'non-academic' or 'disaffected' or 'disengaged'. Now, *A Curriculum for Excellence* is promoting 'cross-cutting themes' and there is a suggestion that inter-disciplinary learning should, for all learners and at all stages of their education, sit alongside subjects as a way of exploring ideas and world events. How could a child meaningfully study, for example, global warming, if only from the perspective, say, of Physics? How could the effect of the tsunami be understood only in a Geography lesson? How could the culture of Scotland be understood only through History? And is the 'nature and purpose' of mathematics comprehensible only in the Maths classroom?

Initiatives and approaches

Another arena in which connections must be made is that of curricular approaches and programmes. At any one time there are simply too many initiatives for any one teacher to engage in, too many programmes which claim to improve learning and teaching, for any one teacher to implement. So connections need to be made. As we have seen, individual Local Authorities in Scotland have taken different approaches to this issue. In Highland Council, Kevin Logan has led a concerted effort over a number of years to promote effective learning and teaching from a thinking skills perspective. More recently, Assessment is for Learning has become the focus, but still from a thinking skills perspective, with connections being made to *teaching for understanding, cooperative learning, rich tasks* and other perspectives.

Theory, research and practice

The CPD programme which Kevin Logan runs in Highland Council Local Authority is supported by impressive, research-led resources. In this way another set of connections is made among theory, research and practice. Vygotsky is never far away from the discussions which inform practice, and the work of Feuerstein, Limpan, Buzan, Gardner, Perkins and others informs the debate about effective learning and teaching. The commitment to research has involved both practitioner-led work as part of the Assessment is for Learning programme as well as larger-scale evaluations of work funded by central Government. In the past, there was an uneasy relationship among theory, research and practice (Boyd, 2005); now, partly because of the impact of *Inside the Black Box* – a research-based publication – and partly because of developments in Scotland including *A Teaching Profession for the 21st Century* – enshrining professional reading as an element of CPD – and *A Curriculum for Excellence* – with its emphasis on pedagogy – teachers are more able to reflect upon and review their practice in the light of theory and research.

So what will the learning classroom look like?

Making sense of all of the advice on how to make learning and teaching more effective is a real challenge for the classroom teacher. A Curriculum for Excellence (ACfE) clearly stated that the curriculum is 'concerned both with what is to be learned and *how it is taught*'. Thus, *pedagogy*, the theory and practice of teaching, is at the heart of the curriculum.

Each of the four purposes of the curriculum outlined in *A Curriculum for Excellence* has a short list of characteristics which should be the starting point for all learning and teaching:

Successful learners have:
• enthusiasm for learning
• determination to reach high standards of achievement
• openness to new thinking and ideas.

Confident individuals have:
• self-respect
• a sense of physical, mental and emotional wellbeing
• secure values and beliefs
• ambition.

Responsible citizens have:
• respect for others
• commitment to participate responsibly in political, economic and cultural life.

Effective contributors have:
• an enterprising attitude
• resilience
• self-reliance.

The question is whether the learning classroom, as outlined above, will enable these characteristics to flourish.

The early part of the twenty-first century has seen the biggest school building programme since the 1960s. Using variants of the New Labour Government's *Private Finance Initiative (PFI)* or *Public Private Partnership (PPP)*, most Local Authorities embarked on building programmes, starting with secondary schools and moving on to primaries. To say that there has been an opportunity missed would be an understatement. Many of these buildings have been built with *efficiency* rather than *effectiveness* in mind, with more emphasis on profit and return on private investment than innovation in design and creativity in layout. Keir Bloomer, former Director of Education in Clackmannanshire, has drawn the comparison between the opulence and design quality of shopping malls such as Prince's Square in Glasgow and the functionalism of the average new school building. He has suggested that there is an implicit message about the value placed on public education by such a contrast, and this is borne out by examples from across the country of new schools being built with only one electronic whiteboard for 1,800 pupils, with only one lifting device for a large special needs school for secondary-age pupils, with classrooms which are simply too small and with public spaces which are all, of necessity, multi-purpose. There are, it must be said, some notable exceptions to this bleak picture. A small number of secondary schools, either in Local Authorities which eschewed PFI or which supplemented funding from their own coffers, and some primary schools, have been designed with input from the people who use them. The best example to date is in Glasgow, a school for young people with additional support needs. Here, the consultation process was thorough, the building was designed to be in harmony with its immediate environment (in this case a public park) and the materials used and the layout were designed specifically with educational and social aims in mind.

Physical layout of the learning classroom

I have argued in Chapter 1 that the classroom of the early twenty-first century is still instantly recognisable as a classroom. However, there have been huge changes in technology and in the materials available for school designers. Classrooms are carpeted, furniture is more flexible in its uses, LCD projectors and laptop computers are now affordable, and so on. So what should a classroom look like in the twenty-first century?

It should be flexible, with furniture which allows for a range of different configurations. It may or may not require a teacher's desk but, even it if does, the desk won't be the focal point. There needs to be the possibility of adapting the layout to suit the purposes of the lesson, so that, when cooperation is needed, pupils can sit in groups; when there is a whole-class debate or a mock trial, or pupils are presenting their work to the rest of the class using the LCD projector and/or electronic whiteboard, then the rest of the class can be in audience mode.

The classroom should be attractive. It always amuses me that when I comment favourably on a primary classroom, its attractiveness, its wall displays (always double mounted), its organisation of resources, its celebration of pupils' work and so on, I often get self-deprecating comments from the teacher, apologetic about a panel of the wall which hasn't been changed in two months. I have to stop myself from replying 'why don't you come with me to the secondary school and I'll show you wall displays which haven't changed in 30 years'. The physical aspects of the classroom are not an irrelevance; they contribute to the classroom culture. Many secondary teachers know this and some classrooms are spectacular, imaginatively and thoughtfully arranged so as to enhance the learning experiences which take place in them. But there are too many others which are dull, unwelcoming and untidy. It is sad to have to say that the new schools being built in the secondary sectors have often done little to encourage teachers to create classrooms that rival those in primaries. Indeed, in the interests of *efficiency*, teachers may be peripatetic, like the pupils, and the sense of belonging, which is part of the primary ethos, is lost.

The classroom should be, above all, designed for learning. Resources should be readily available and organised in a way that allows pupils to take responsibility for them. Routines are an important aspect of classroom life and these can help establish the calm, purposeful and orderly environment which is conducive both to good order and to productive learning. The pace of learning, time-on-task and engagement are all influenced by the surroundings. Teachers who personalise their classrooms, who use the physical cues to signal the kind of ethos they wish to create, who involve the pupils in the process, are more likely to be thoughtful in their pedagogy. The teachers *without limits* featured in the Hart *et al.* study (2004) were notably concerned to create attractive learning environments. The best modern school buildings are those which are the result of lengthy consultation with all stakeholders, including pupils and teachers.

Endnote

At the time of writing, there are promising signs that Scottish teachers are willing to discuss, and ask questions of, some of the big ideas considered in this book. Many of the people whose work has been referred to – Gardner, Perkins, Feuerstein, Buzan, Hannaford, Costa, Dweck, Fisher and Wiliam – have been to Scotland recently, most of them under the auspices of Tapestry, an organisation dedicated to promoting creativity in education. Indeed, when Howard Gardner came to Glasgow in 2006, 1,300 people attended the conference to hear this Harvard academic talk about his latest book, *Five Minds for the Future*. It was he, too, who said at an earlier, two-day conference featuring a number of contributors 'If you have agreed with everything you have heard over the last two days, then you haven't been listening.' Education is a complex endeavour; there are no easy answers, no quick fixes. If there were, someone would have found them by now. We need to continue to make the best use of what we know and apply it in the best ways we can. As Edwin Morgan wrote, in a different context:

> Deplore what is to be deplored,
> And then find out the rest.
>
> (Edwin Morgan, 'King Billy')

POINTS FOR REFLECTION

1 Do you agree with the 10 principles as laid out in the conclusion of this book?

2 How would you use these 10 principles to engage your colleagues in a discussion about *the learning classroom?*

3 Could these principles form the basis of classroom observation and shared practice within and across schools?

References

Chapter 1

Alexander, R. (2004, 2006) *Towards Dialogic Teaching: Rethinking Classroom Talk* Dialogos. Accessed from: www.robinalexander.org.uk

Black, P and Wiliam, D. (1998) *Inside the Black Box: Raising Standards Through Classroom Assessment* London: Kings College

Boyd, B. (1979) *Beginning Group Work in S1* Edinburgh: Scottish Curriculum Development Centre

Boyd, B. (2005) *Primary–Secondary Transition* Paisley: Hodder Gibson

Cohen, L., Mannion, L. and Morrison, K. (1996) *A Guide to Teaching Practice* London: Routledge

Dweck, C. S. (1999) *Self-Theories: Their Role in Motivation, Personality, and Development* Philadelphia, PA: Psychology Press

Fisher, R. (1990) *Teaching Children to Think* Cheltenham: Nelson Thornes

Fitz-gibbon, C. T. (1997) *Value Added National Project: Final Report* London: School Curriculum and Assessment Authority Publications

Flanders, N. (1970) *Analysing Teacher Behaviour* Reading, MA: Addison Wesley

Galton, M. (2007) *Learning and Teaching in the Primary Classroom* London: Sage

Hamill, P. and Boyd, B. (2001) Rhetoric or reality: inter-agency provision for young people with challenging behaviour *Emotional and Behavioural Difficulties* Vol. 6, No. 3

Hamill, P. and Boyd, B. (2003) Interviews with young people about behaviour support – equality, fairness and rights in inclusive education: learners and learning contexts, in

M. Nind, K. Sheehy and K. Simmons (eds) *Inclusive Education: Learners and Learning Contexts*, Part 3 Chapter 12 (pp. 123–136) London: David Fulton

Hart, S., Dixon, A., Drummond, M. J. and McIntyre, D. (2004) *Learning without Limits* Maidenhead, Berkshire: Open University Press

Her Majesty's Inspectorate of Education *(2007) How Good is our School?* Edinburgh

Johnson, D. and Johnson, R. (1990) *Cooperation and Competition: Theory and Research* Edina, MN: Interaction Book Company

Kyriacou, C. (2001) *Essential Teaching Skills* Cheltenham: Nelson Thornes

MacBeath, J., Boyd, B., Rand, J. and Bell, S. (1996) *Schools Speak for Themselves* National Union of Teachers England and Wales

McLean, A. (2003) *The Motivated School* London: Paul Chapman Publishing

Mosley, J. (1998) *Turn Your School Around: a circle time approach to the development of self-esteem and positive behaviour in the primary staffroom, classroom and playground* Wisbech, Cambridgeshire: LDA

Rudduck, J., Caplin, R. and Wallace, G. (1996) *School Effectiveness: What Can Pupils Tell Us?* London: David Fulton

Schön, D. (1983) *The Reflective Practitioner: How Professionals Think in Action* London: Temple Smith

Scottish Education Department (1965) *The Primary Memorandum* Edinburgh

Scottish Executive Education Department (1999) *National Priorities* Edinburgh

Scottish Executive Education Department (2004) *A Curriculum for Excellence* Edinburgh

Scottish Executive Education Department (2006) *A Curriculum for Excellence: Progress and Proposals* Edinburgh

University of Bristol (2008) *This Learning Life* Proceedings of Conference held in May 2007

Watkins, C. (2005) *Classrooms as Learning Communities: What's in it for Schools?* Abingdon: Routledge

Wragg, E. C. (1989) *Classroom Teaching Skills* London: Routledge

Wragg, E. C. (1993) *Primary Teaching Skills* London: Routledge

Wragg, E. C. (1994) *An Introduction to Classroom Observation* London and New York: Routledge

Chapter 2

Adams, M. (2007) *Denial worse than the abuse,* Times Educational Supplement Scotland Friday 16 November

Boyd, B. (2005) *Primary–Secondary Transition* Paisley: Hodder Gibson

Coffield, F., Mosely, D., Hall, E. and Ecclestone, K. (2004) *Learning Styles and Pedagogy in Post-16 Learning: A Systematic and Critical Review* London: DES

Cohen, L., Mannion, L. and Morrison, K. (1996) *A Guide to Teaching Practice* London: Routledge

Department of Education and Science (1989) *Discipline in Schools* (The Elton Report) London: HMSO

Good, T. L. and Brophy, J. E. (1974) 'The influence of teachers' attitudes and expectations on classroom behaviour' in R.H. Coop and K. White (eds) *Psychological Concepts in the Classroom* New York: Harper and Row

Hamill, P. and Boyd, B. (2001) Rhetoric or reality: inter-agency provision for young people with challenging behaviour *Emotional and Behavioural Difficulties* Vol. 6 (3)

Hamill, P. and Boyd, B. (2003) Interviews with young people about behaviour support – equality, fairness and rights in inclusive education: learners and learning contexts, in M. Nind, K. Sheehy and K. Simmons (eds), *Inclusive Education: Learners and Learning Contexts,* Part 3 Chapter 12 (pp. 123–136) London: David Fulton

Kagan, S., Kyle, P. and Scott, S. (2004) *Win-Win Discipline* San Clemente: Kagan Publishing

Kyriacou, C. (2007) *Essential Teaching Skills* 3rd edition Cheltenham: Nelson Thornes

MacBeath, J., Boyd, B., Rand, J. and Bell, S. (1996) *Schools Speak for Themselves* Glasgow: University of Strathclyde

McIlvanney, W. (1975) *Docherty* Edinburgh: Mainstream

McLean, A (2003) *The Motivated School* London: Paul Chapman Publishing

Mosley, J. (1998) *Turn Your School Around: a circle time approach to the development of self-esteem and positive behaviour in the primary staffroom, classroom and playground* Wisbech, Cambridgeshire: LDA

Scottish Education Department (1977) *Truancy and Indiscipline in Scottish Schools* (The Pack Report) Edinburgh: HMSO

Scottish Executive Education Department (2004) *A Curriculum for Excellence* Edinburgh

Scottish Executive Education Department (2001) *Better Behaviour, Better Learning – Report of the Discipline Task Force* Edinburgh

Chapter 3

Black, P. and Wiliam, D. (1998) *Inside the Black Box: Raising Standards Through Classroom Assessment* London: Kings College

Black, P. and Wiliam, D. (1998b) Assessment and classroom learning *Assessment in Education* March, pp. 7–71

Clark, S. (2006) *Unlocking Formative Assessment* London: Hodder and Stoughton

Dweck, C. S. (1999) *Self-Theories: Their Role in Motivation, Personality, and Development* Philadelphia, PA: Psychology Press

Fisher, R. (1990) *Teaching Children to Think* Cheltenham: Nelson Thornes; Oxford: Blackwell

Flanders, N. (1970) *Analysing Teacher Behaviour* Reading, MA: Addison Wesley

Highland Council www.hvlc.org.uk/ace/aifl/

Chapter 4

Alexander, R. (2004, 2006) *Towards Dialogic Teaching* Dialogos Accessed from: www.robinalexander.org.uk

Black, P and Wiliam, D. (1998) *Inside the Black Box: Raising Standards Through Classroom Assessment* London: Kings College

Boyd, B. and Simpson, M. (2000) *Developing a Framework for Effective Learning and Teaching in S1 and S2 in Angus Secondary Schools* Angus Council

Bruner, J. (1977) *The Process of Education* Cambridge, MA: Harvard University Press

Buzan, T. (1993) *The Mind Map Book: Radiant Thinking* London: BBC Books

Consultative Committee on the Curriculum (1986) *Education 10–14 in Scotland: Report of the Programme Directing Committee* Dundee College of Education

Covey, S. (1989) *Seven Habits of Highly Effective People* New York: Free Press

De Bono, E. (1973) *The CORT Thinking Programme* Oxford: Pergamon

Eisner, E. W. (1985) *The Art of Educational Evaluation: A Personal View* Barcombe: Falmer

Entwistle, N. (2000) Promoting deep learning through teaching and assessment: conceptual frameworks and educational concepts. Paper presented to Teaching and Learning Research Programme conference, Leicester, November 2000. Accessed from: www.tlrp.org/acadpub/Entwistle2000.pdf

Feuerstein, R. and Jensen, M.R. (1980) *Instrumental enrichment: an intervention programme for cognitive modifiability* Baltimore, MD: University Park Press

Fisher, R. (1990) *Teaching Children to Think* Cheltenham: Stanley Thornes

Furth and Wachs (1974) *Thinking Goes to School* Oxford: Oxford University Press

Gardner, H. (1983) *Frames of Mind: The Theory of Multiple Intelligences* New York: Basic Books

Goleman, D. (1996) *Emotional Intelligence* London: Bloomsbury

Hannaford, C. (1995) *Smart Moves: Why Learning is Not All Inside Your Head* Hawaii: Jumilla Nur Publishing

Kirkwood, M. (2005) *Learning to Think: Thinking to Learn* Paisley: Hodder Gibson

Lipman, M. (2003) *Thinking in Education*, 2nd edition, Cambridge: Cambridge University Press

McGuinness, C. (1999) *From thinking skills to thinking classrooms: A review and evaluation of approaches for developing pupils' thinking* London HMSO

Perkins, D. (1995) *Smart Schools: Better Thinking and Learning for Every Child* New York: The Free Press

Scottish Consultative Council on the Curriculum (1980) *English Language 5–14* Edinburgh: HMSO

Vygotsky, L. S. (1978) *Mind in Society: The Development of Higher Psychological Processes* Cambridge, MA: Harvard University Press

Chapter 5

Bandura, A. (1997) *Self-efficacy: The exercise of control* New York: W.H. Freeman

Black, P. and Wiliam, D. (1998) *Inside the Black Box: Raising Standards Through Classroom Assessment* London: King's College

Boyd, B. (2005) *Primary-Secondary Translation* Paisley: Hodder Gibson

Boyd, B. and Lawson, J. (2004) Guidance matters: A pupil perspective on guidance with a Scottish Council *Improving Schools* Vol. 7, No. 2, pp. 171–184

Brophy, J. (1987) Socialising student motivation to learn, in M. L. Maehr and D. A. Kleiber (eds), *Advances in Motivation and Achievement, Vol. 5 Enhancing Motivation* Greenwich, CT: JAI Press Inc.

Brown, S and McIntyre, D. (1993). *Making Sense of Teaching* Buckingham: Open University Press

Buzan, T. (1993) *The Mind Map Book: Radiant Thinking* London: BBC Books

Consultative Committee on the Curriculum (1986) *Education 10–14 in Scotland: Report of the Programme Directing Committee* Dundee College of Education

Corno, L. (1986) Self regulated learning and classroom teaching (Paper presented at the annual meeting of the American Educational Research Association in San Francisco)

Craig, C. (2003) *The Scots' Crisis of Confidence* Edinburgh: Big Thinking

Craig, C. (2007) *Creating Confidence: A Handbook for Professionals Working with Young People* Glasgow: Centre for Confidence and Wellbeing

Dweck, C. S. (1999) *Self-Theories: Their Role in Motivation, Personality and Development* Philadelphia: Taylor and Frances Psychology Press

Education Act 1872

Entwistle, N. J. (1987) Motivation to learn: Conceptualisations and practicalities *British Journal of Educational Studies* Vol. 35, No. 2, pp.129–148

Furedi, F. (2003) *Therapy Culture* London: Routledge

Kozeki, B. (1985) Motives and motivational styles in education, in N. J. Entwistle (ed.) *New Directions in Educational Psychology Vol. 1 Learning and Teaching* Lewes: Falmer Press

Leary, M.R., Tambor, E.S.W., Terdal, S.K. and Chokel, J.T. (1995) Self-esteem as an interpersonal monitor: the sociometer hypothesis *Journal of Personality and Social Psychology*, 74, 1290–1299.

MacBeath, J. and Mortimore, P. (Eds) (2001) *Improving School Effectiveness*, Buckingham: Open University Press

Marton, F. and Saljo, R. (1984) Approaches to learning, in F. Marton, D. J. Hounsell and N. J. Entwistle (eds) *The Experience of Learning* Edinburgh: The Scottish Academic Press

Maslow, A. H. (1970) *Motivation and Personality: Second Edition* New York: Harper and Row

McLean, A. (2003) *The Motivated School* London: Sage

McLean, A (2008, forthcoming) *Promoting Motivational Resilience* London: Sage

Nisbet, J. D. and Schucksmith, J. (1986) *Learning Strategies* London: Routledge and Kegan Paul

Perkins, D. (1993) Teaching for understanding *American Educator* Vol. 17, No. 3, pp. 28–35

Perkins, D. (1995) *Smart Schools: Better Thinking and Learning for Every Child* New York: Free Press

Rollett, B. (1987) Effort avoidance and learning, in E. DeCorte, H. Lodewijks, R. Parmentier and P. Span (eds) *Learning and Instruction* Oxford: Pergamon

Rudduck, J., Chaplain, R. and Wallace, G. (eds) (1996) *School Improvement: What Can Pupils Tell Us?* London: David Fulton Publishers

Seligman, M. E. P., Reivich, K., Jaycox, L. and Gillahm, J. (1995) *The Optimistic Child* New York: Harper Perennial

Twenge, J. (2006) *Generation Me* New York: Free Press

Weiner, B. (1984) Attribution theory in personality psychology in L. Pervin (ed) *Handbook of personality: theory and research* (pp. 465–485) New York: Guilford

Chapter 6

Advisory Council on Education (1944) *Training for Citizenship* Edinburgh: Scottish Education Department

Baginsky, M. and Hannam, D. (1999) *School Councils: The Views of Students and Teachers* London: NCPCC

Bandura, A. (1986) *Social Foundations of Thought and Action: A Social Cognitive Theory* Englewood Cliffs, NJ: Prentice-Hall

Boyd, B. (2005) *Primary–Secondary Transition* Paisley: Hodder Gibson

Bruner, J. (1977) *The Process of Education* Cambridge, MA: Harvard University Press

Deuchar, R. (2007) *Citizenship, Enterprise and Learning* Stoke on Trent: Trentham Books

Dewey, J. (1915) *The School and Society* Chicago, IL: The University of Chicago Press

Learning and Teaching Scotland (2002) *Education for Citizenship in Scotland: A Paper for Discussion and Development* Glasgow www.ltscotland.org.uk/citizenship/index.asp

Maitles, H., Cowan, P. and Butler, E. (2005) *Never Again! Does Holocaust Education have an Effect on Pupils' Citizenship Values and Attitudes* Edinburgh: Scottish Executive Social Research

Marks, S. (2000) *The Riddle of all Constitutions* Oxford: Oxford University Press

Money, R. (2007) Pride and Prejudice, *The Sunday Herald* (Sunday 16.12.07)

Philips, D.C. and Soltis, J.F. (2004) *Perspectives on Learning* New York: Teachers College Press

Rousseau, J.J. (1762) *The Social Contract or Principles of Political Right*, trans. G. D. H. Cole, Rendered into HTML and text by Jon Roland of the Constitution Society

Scottish Education Department (1944) *Training for Citizenship: A Report of the Advisory Council on Education in Scotland* Edinburgh: HMSO

Scottish Executive Education Department (2001) *A Teaching Profession for the 21st Century (The McCrone Report)* Edinburgh: HMSO

Short, G. and Reed, C.A. (2004) *Issues in Holocaust Education* Hampshire: Ashgate

Chapter 7

Ball, C. (1984) Educating for enterprise: the overseas experience, in A.G. Watts and P. Moran (eds) *Education for Enterprise* Cambridge: CRAC Publications

Centre for Studies in Enterprise, Career Development and Work (Enterprising Careers) (2005) *The Enterprising School* Glasgow: University of Strathclyde

Centre for Studies in Enterprise, Career Development and Work (Enterprising Careers) (2007) *Enterprising Ideas for Secondary Schools* Glasgow: University of Strathclyde

Deuchar, R. (2007) *Citizenship, Enterprise and Learning* Stoke on Trent: Trentham Books

Feuerstein, R., Feuerstein, R.S., Falik, L.H. and Rand, Y. (2002) *The Dynamic Assessment of Cognitive Modifiability* Jerusalem: International Centre for the Enhancement of Learning Potential

Fisher, R. (2001) *Teaching Children to Think* Cheltenham: Nelson Thornes

Gardner, H., Csikszentmihalyi, M. and Damon, W. (2001) *Good Work* New York: Basic Books

Office of Curriculum Education (2005) *Rich Tasks 2005* Report of Rich Tasks Team Queensland Australia

Oliver, D. and Heater, D. (1994) *The Foundations of Citizenship* New York: Harvester Wheatsheaf

Scottish Executive Education Department (2002) *Determined to Succeed: A Review of Enterprise Education* Accessed from: www.determinedtosucceed.co.uk

Scottish Executive (2001) *Smart, Successful Scotland: Ambitions for the Enterprise Network* Edinburgh: HMSO

Scottish Executive (2002) *Global Entrepreneurship Monitor, Scotland* Glasgow: University of Strathclyde

Shacklock , G., Hattam, R. and Smyth, J. (2000) Enterprise education and teachers' work: exploring the links *Journal of Education and Work* Vol. 13, No. 1, pp. 41–58

South Lanarkshire Council (2007) *Learning and Teaching Strategies for A Curriculum for Excellence* Blantyre Education Resources

Chapter 8

Barker, A. (2003) Bottom: A Case Study Comparing Teaching Low Ability and Mixed Ability Year 9 English Classes *English in Education* Vol 37 No 1 NATE

Boaler, J., Wlliam, D. and Brown, M. (2000) Students' experiences of ability grouping – Disaffection, polarisation and the construction of failure *British Educational Research Journal*, Vol. 26, No. 5, pp. 631–648

Boyd, B. (2005) *Primary–Secondary Transition* Paisley: Hodder Gibson

Boyd, B. (2007) To set or not to set; is that the question? *Improving Schools* Vol 10 No 2 pp. 223-234 Sage Publications

Eliot, T. S. (1948) *Notes Towards a Definition of Culture* London: Faber & Faber

Feuerstein, R., Feuerstein, R.S., Falik, L.H. and Rand, Y. (2002) *The Dynamic Assessment of Cognitive Modifiability* Jerusalem: International Centre for the Enhancement of Learning Potential

Findley, W. and Bryan, M. (1971) *Ability Grouping, 1970: Status, Impact and Alternatives* Athens, GA: Center for Educational Improvement

Gow, L. and McPherson, A. (1980) *Tell Them from Me* Aberdeen: Aberdeen University Press

Hallam, S. and Ireson, J. (2005) Secondary school teachers' pedagogic practices when teaching mixed and structured ability classes *Research Papers in Education*, Vol. 20, No.1 pp. 3–24

Hallam, S. and Ireson, J. (2006) Secondary school pupils' preferences for different types of structured grouping practices *British Educational Research Journal*, Vol. 32, No. 4, August 2006, pp. 583–599

Harlen, W. and Malcolm H. (1997) *Setting and Streaming: A Research Review* Edinburgh: SCRE

Hart, S., Dixon, A., Drummond, M. J. and McIntyre, D. (2004) *Learning without Limits* Buckingham: Open University Press

Ireson, J., Hallam, S., and Plewis, I. (2001) *Ability grouping in secondary schools: effects on pupils' self-concepts* British Journal of Educational Psychology, *71*, 2, 315–326.

Ireson J., Clark H. and Hallam S. (2002) Constructing ability groups in the secondary school: issues in practice *School Leadership and Management* Vol.22, No. 2, pp. 163–176

Ireson, J., Hallam, S. and Hurley, C. (2005) What are the effects of ability grouping on GCSE attainment? *British Educational Research Journal* Vol. 31, No. 4, pp. 443–458

Kutnick, P., Blatchford, P., Clark, H., MacIntyre, H. and Baines, E. (2005) Teachers' understandings of the relationship between within-class (student) grouping and learning in secondary schools *Educational Research*, Vol. 47, No. 1, pp. 1–24

McGuire M., Woolridge T. and Pratt-Adams, S. (2006) *The Urban Primary School* Buckingham: Open University Press

Smith, C.M.M. and Sutherland, M.J. (2006) Setting or mixed ability: pupils' views of organisational arrangements in their school *Journal of Research in Special Needs Education*, Vol. 6, No. 2, p. 69

Chapter 9

Adey, P. and Shayer, M. (1994) *Really Raising Standards: Cognitive Intervention and Academic Achievement* London: Routledge

Alexander, R. (2005) Culture, dialogue and learning: notes on an emerging pedagogy, in *Education, Culture and Cognition: Intervening for Growth* Conference of the International Association for Cognitive Education and Psychology, University of Durham, July

Alexander, R. (2006) [2004] *Towards Dialogic Teaching: Rethinking Classroom Talk* Dialogos Accessed from: www.robinalexander.org.uk

Black, P. and Wiliam, D. (1998) *Inside the Black Box: Raising Standards Through Classroom Assessment* London: King's College

Boyd, B. (2005) *Primary–Secondary Transition* Paisley: Hodder Gibson

Boyd, B. and Lawson, J. (2007) *Talking, Listening and Learning in Inverclyde* Glasgow: University of Strathclyde

Boyd, B. and Simpson, M. (2000) *Developing a Framework for Effective Learning and Teaching in S1 and S2 in Angus Secondary Schools* Arbroath: Angus Council

Feuerstein, R. (1990) Mediating cognitive processes to the retarded performer – rationale, goals and nature of intervention, in M. Schwebel and N. Fagley (eds) *Promoting Cognitve Growth over the Life Span: Proceedings of the Third Annual Rutgers University Graduate School of Applied and Professional Psychology Conference: Thinking and Learning Skills*, pp. 115–136, Hillsdale NJ: Erlbaum

Her Majesty's Inspectors of Schools (1996) *Achievement for All* Edinburgh: HMSO

Johnson, D., and Johnson, R. (1990) *Cooperation and Competition: Theory and Research* Edina, MN: Interaction Book Company

Johnson, D., Johnson, R. and Smith, K. (1991) *Active Learning: Cooperation in the College Classroom* Edina, MN: Interaction Book Company, cited in Ward, C. and Craigen, J. (1999) *Cooperative Learning: A Resource Booklet* Ontario, Canada

Kozulin, A. (1994) The cognitive revolution in learning, in J. N. Mangieri and C. C. Block (eds) *Creating Powerful Thinking in Teachers and Students: Diverse Perspectives* pp. 269–287, Fort Worth, TX: Harcourt Brace Publishers

Mobilia, W. and Gordon, R. (1997) *Education by Design: The Level 1 Coaching Kit* New Hampshire: Antioch University

Nystrand, M. with Gamoran, A., Kachur, R and Prendergast, C. (1997) *Opening Dialogue: Understanding the Dynamics of Language and Learning in the English Classroom* New York: Teachers College Press

Perkins, D. (1995) *Smart Schools: Better Thinking and Learning for Every Child* New York: Free Press

Scottish Education Department (1965) *Primary Education in Scotland (The Primary Memorandum)* Edinburgh: HMSO

Ward, C and Craigen, J. (1999) *Cooperative Learning: A Resource Booklet* Ontario, Canada: Durham District School Board

Chapter 10

Bruner, J. (1996) *The Culture of Education* Cambridge, MA: Harvard University Press

Christie, D. (2007) Lecture to PGDE (Secondary) students at the University of Strathclyde

Coffield, F., Mosely, D., Hall, E. and Ecclestone, K. (2004) *Learning Styles and Pedagogy in Post-16 Learning: A Systematic and Critical Review* London: DES

Dweck, C. (2007) Address to Conference organised by the Centre for Confidence and Wellbeing held in June in Oran Mor, Glasgow

Dweck, C. S. (1999) *Self-Theories: Their Role in Motivation, Personality, and Development* Philadelphia, PA: Psychology Press

Economic and Social Research Council (2002) *Neuroscience and Education: Issues and Opportunities*

Eliot, T. S. (1948) *Notes Towards a Definition of Culture* London: Faber & Faber

Feuerstein, R., Feuerstein, R. S., Falik, L. H. and Rand, Y. (2002) *The Dynamic Assessment of Cognitive Modifiability* Jerusalem: ICELP Press

Gardner, M. (1983) *Frames of Mind: The Theory of Multiple Intelligences* New York: Basic Books

Goleman, D. (1996) *Emotional Intelligence* London: Bloomsbury

Hall, J. (2005) *Neuroscience and Education: What can Brain Science Contribute to Learning and Teaching* Spotlight Research Report 121, Glasgow: Scottish Council for Research in Education

Hannaford, C. (2002) *Awakening the Child Heart* Hawaii: Jamilla Nur Publishing

Hannaford, C. (2005) *Smart Moves: Why Learning is Not All in your Head* Utah: Great River Books

Hart, S., Dixon, A., Drummond, M. J. and McIntyre, D. (2004) *Learning without Limits* Maidenhead, Berkshire: Open University Press

Scottish Borders Council (2005) Leaflets on Emotional Intelligence produced by A-T Lawrie, Development Officer, in support of Learning and Teaching CPD

The Scottish Network on Able Pupils (SNAP) Newsletter (Issue 23, Spring 2004)

Sternberg, R. (1990) *Metaphors of Mind: Conceptions of the Nature of Intelligence* New York: Cambridge University Press

Chapter 11

Boyd, B. (2005) *Primary–Secondary Transition* Paisley: Hodder Gibson

Bruner, J.S. (1960) *The Process of Education* Cambridge, MA: Harvard University Press

Learning and Teaching Scotland (2007) *The Global Dimension in the Curriculum* Glasgow: Learning and Teaching Scotland

Lipman, M. (1982) Philosophy for children *Thinking: The Journal of Philosophy for Children* Vol. 3, pp. 35–44

Phillips, D.C. and Soltis, J.F. (2004) *Perspectives on Learning* New York: Teachers College Press

Regan, C. (ed.) (2006) *80:20 Development in an Unequal World* Ireland: 80:20 Educating and Acting for a Better World

Shepherd, J. (2007) What does Britain expect? *Guardian* (Tuesday 17.07.07)

Smith, E. (2007) Johnny causes storm in lecture on climate change *Times Educational Supplement Scotland* (21 December 2007)

Conclusion

Black, P. and Wiliam, D. (1998) *Inside the Black Box: Raising Standards Through Classroom Assessment* London: King's College

Boyd, B. (2005) *Primary–Secondary Transition* Paisley: Hodder Gibson

Boyd, B. and Simpson, M. (2000) *Developing a Framework for Effective Learning and Teaching in S1 and S2 in Angus Secondary Schools* Arbroath: Angus Council

Csikszentmihalyi, M. (1991) *Flow: the psychology of optimal experience* New York: HarperCollins

Gardner, H. (2006) *Five Minds for the Future* Boston, MA: Harvard Business School Press

Hart, S., Dixon, A., Drummond, M. J. and McIntyre, D. (2004) *Learning without Limits* Maidenhead, Berkshire: Open University Press

MacBeath, J., Boyd, B., Rand, J. and Bell, S. (1996) *Schools Speak for Themselves* National Union of Teachers England and Wales

Perkins, D. (1995) *Smart Schools: Better Thinking and Learning for Every Child* New York: Free Press

Scottish Executive Education Department (2004) *A Curriculum for Excellence* Edinburgh

Vygotsky, L.S. (1962) *Thought and Language* Cambridge, MA: MIT Press

Further reading

Amidon, E. and Giammatteo, M. (1965) The verbal behavior of superior teachers *The Elementary School Journal* Vol. 65, No. 5, pp. 283–285

Bryce, T.G.K. and Humes, W.M. (eds) (2008) *Scottish Education* 3rd edn, Edinburgh: Edinburgh University Press

Eisner, E. W. (1998) *The Enlightened Eye: Qualitative Inquiry and the Enhancement of Educational Practice* Upper Saddle River, NJ: Prentice Hall

Feuerstein, R., Feuerstein, R. S., Falik, L. H. and Rand, Y. (2002) *The Dynamic Assessment of Cognitive Modifiability* Jerusalem: ICELP Press

Fisher, R. and Williams, M. (eds) (2004) *Unlocking Creativity* London: David Fulton Publishers

Jarvis, P., Holford, J. and Griffin, C. (1999) *The Theory and Practice of Learning* London: Kogan Page

Galton, M. (2007) *Learning and Teaching in the Primary Classroom* London: Sage Publications

Gardner, H. (2006) *Changing Minds* Boston, MA: Harvard Business School Press

Gardner, H. and Jie-Qi, S. (eds) (2008) *MI around the World* New York: Jossey-Bass

Hills, G. and Nicol, I. (2005) *Education for the 21st Century* London: RSA

Learning and Teaching Scotland (1999) *The Reggio Emilia Approach to Early Years Education* Glasgow

McGregor, D. (2007) *Developing Thinking; Developing Learning* Maidenhead, Berkshire: Open University Press

Queensland Government Department of Education and the Arts (2004) *New Basic: Rich Tasks*

Scottish Education Department (1944) *Training for Citizenship: A Report of the Advisory Council on Education in Scotland* Edinburgh: HMSO

South Lanarkshire Council (2007) *Developing Thinking: Staff Development DVD*.

Wrigley, T. (2006) *Another School is Possible* London: Trentham Books

Index